Basic Moral Concepts

Professor Robert Spaemann's *Basic Moral Concepts* is an excellent introduction to ethical thinking. It deals in a lucid and informative way with vital questions like the relativity of good and evil, justice and self-interest, responsibility, utilitarianism, and the role of the individual in society. Spaemann approaches these and other issues from a point of view refreshingly different from that of many philosophers in the Anglo-Saxon tradition. An important aspect of the book is the impressive battery of arguments he brings to bear against the sort of facile relativism which all too easily passes for ethical thought.

Writing clearly and without jargon, Professor Spaemann provides a stimulating discussion of the fundamental concepts we use every day when we deliberate, either alone or with others, about the moral aspects of our action. His book will appeal to non-philosophers interested in moral questions and will be indispensable to students of philosophy embarking upon a study of ethics.

'Spaemann has a very clear head and style, and manages to make quite difficult matters intelligible. He is half-way between a popular and a very academic writer, his style making him quite accessible to non-philosophers while his content is of interest to professional philosophers.'

G. E. M. Anscombe, University of Cambridge

The Author

Robert Spaemann is [Professor] of Philosophy at the University of Munich.

Basic Moral Concepts

Robert Spaemann

Translated by T. J. Armstrong

ROUTLEDGE

LONDON AND NEW YORK

First published in Germany as *Moralische Grundbegriffe*
Copyright © C. H. Beck'sche Verlagsbuchhandlung
(Oscar Beck), München 1982

English translation first published 1989 by Routledge
11 New Fetter Lane, London EC4P 4EE
29 West 35th Street, New York, NY 10001

Typeset in 10/12 Baskerville by Columns of Reading

Printed in Great Britain by Cox & Wyman Ltd
Reading, Berks

British Library Cataloguing in Publication Data
Spaemann, Robert
Basic moral concepts
1. Moral philosophy
I. Title   II. Moralische Grundbegriffe. *English*
170

ISBN 0–415–04160–0
ISBN 0–415–02966–X (Pbk)

Library of Congress Cataloging in Publication Data
Spaemann, Robert.
[Moralische Grundbegriffe. English]
Basic moral concepts/Robert Spaemann; translated by
T. J. Armstrong.
p.   cm.
Translation of: Moralische Grundbegriffe.
1. Ethics.   I. Title.
BJ1114.S5413   1989
170—dc19   89–3493

Contents

Translator's note

In this translation I have tended to follow the traditional practice of translating pronouns referring to persons in philosophical examples using the third person singular masculine. I have done this for purposes of fluency and without any discriminatory intent. The examples are, of course, to be taken as referring to women as well as men. Given that it is hard to break with traditional usage without sounding either awkward or affected, some consolation might be found in the fact that it is in the nature of philosophical examples generally to show up their protagonists in a bad light.

Preface

Some people claim that ethics and morality are self-explanatory. If they are right there is nothing more to say. It is not possible to find more comprehensible ways of explaining what is already self-explanatory. Not even zoological analogies are any use. In the last analysis we only know what grey geese are because of what we know about ourselves, not vice versa.

If something is self-explanatory it can only be pointed out, it cannot be put into words. That is why Ludwig Wittgenstein wrote, 'It is clear that ethics is not something which can be expressed'. Plato was well aware of the fact that it is not possible to give a text-book definition of the word 'good'; 'It is only after frequent and informal discussion directly on the topic, within the setting of our common life, that the Idea springs up in the soul like a light kindled from a spark of fire, which then continues burning of its own accord' (7th letter, 341 C 5).

In fact there is no end to the talk which goes on about this supposedly self-explanatory topic, and this is simply because there is no end to the disagreement over it. There is no 'pure form' of ethics which can be grasped or understood. What actually happens with regard to the ethics of a particular society is never simply self-explanatory. There are always some things which are not known about, pushed to one side, suppressed. So it is always possible to claim that the dominant ethical code in any society is nothing more than the ethical code which happens to suit those in dominant positions, that the only appropriate way to use the word 'good' is to misuse it, and that it is a failure to understand oneself which makes things seem 'self-explanatory'. It is easy enough to demonstrate that none of this is true. But in order to do so, one does have to talk about things which are allegedly self-explanatory.

Rousseau understood the dilemma: 'I would not take it upon myself to try to teach people, if others did not keep on leading them astray.' Teaching can be carried out on different levels. On the most fundamental level one might attempt to trace back what we recognize as moral duties, virtues, norms, or values to a common root, and, whilst doing so, assemble them into a systematic structure. This is the traditional occupation of moral philosophy. On a more applied level, specific questions can be discussed: lying, euthanasia, abortion, military service, questions of sexuality, our relationship with nature, and so on. Up to the time of Kant philosophers and theologians did not consider it beneath their dignity to discuss questions like these. If, in studying moral philosophy, we could not get beyond empty formulae and could learn nothing about how we should live, it would not be an interesting enough subject to be worth tackling.

The eight chapters of this little book are not restricted to either of these two levels. They range over a mid-level of abstraction between fundamental questions and application to individual cases. They discuss some of the fundamental concepts which we use every day if we deliberate, either alone or with others, about the moral aspects of our actions. The aim is to stimulate reflection about these concepts without the use of jargon and without requiring of the reader an academic training in ethics.

The origin of the book was a series of broadcasts for the Bavarian broadcasting authority made in January and February 1981. I have not altered the informal style of these broadcasts. My wish was to get close to the 'frequent and informal' discussion which Plato talks about. The effect which he hoped for can only be produced indirectly, not intentionally.

Robert Spaemann
München 1983

Chapter one

Moral philosophy:
are good and evil relative?

The question of the meaning of the words 'good' and 'evil', 'good' and 'bad', is one of the oldest in philosophy. Yet it is a question which has its place in other subject-areas too. Doctors tell us whether or not we should smoke. Psychologists give advice about career choices, and there are financial advisers to tell us that, for example, now is a good time to open a building society account, because next year the premiums will be worse and waiting times longer. What, one may well ask, has that got to do with ethics or philosophy?

Let us take a closer look at the way the word 'good' is used in these contexts. The doctor says, 'It would be a good idea to spend another day in bed.' To be precise the word 'good' should be qualified in two ways. The doctor should say, 'It is a good idea for you', and 'It is a good idea for you if your first priority is to get well.' These qualifications are important. If for example someone were planning a robbery involving murder for a particular day, then, all things considered, it would doubtless be 'better' if that person picked up a lung infection which would put a stop to his project. Conversely, on a particular day, one of us might have something so pressing and urgent to do that we will disregard the doctor's advice to stay in bed, and take the risk of getting a relapse of influenza. But with regard to the question of whether or not it is 'good' to act in this way, the doctor, as a doctor, can make no pronouncement. From a doctor's point of view 'good' means 'good for you, if your first priority is your health'. That is the doctor's area of responsibility. Whether or not our health should always be our first priority is something about which the doctor can make a pronouncement as a fellow human being, but not in his special capacity as a doctor.

Also, if I decide not to open a building society account but squander the money or give it away to a friend who needs it urgently, then there is nothing my financial adviser can say. For him the word 'good' means 'good for you, if your priority is to increase your wealth in the long term'.

Whenever advice of this nature is given, the word 'good' means something like, 'good for a particular person in some particular respect'. The same course of action could well turn out to be both good and bad, in different respects, for the same person. For example a lot of overtime is good for one's standard of living but bad for one's health. The same thing might well be good for one person and bad for another. The extension of a road might be good for drivers but bad for those living alongside it, and so on.

We use the word 'good' in another sense too, in what one might call an 'absolute' sense, that is, without qualifications like 'for this person' or 'in this respect'. This meaning always comes out when conflict arises between different interests or points of view, even if we are talking about the interests and points of view of one and the same person, as in, for example, the conflict between the viewpoints of standard of living, health and friendship. Here two sorts of questions are present. One sort involves questions like is 'what is really and truly good for me?' or 'what is the correct way of giving an order of priority to the different points of view?' And the other sort is questions like, 'in case of conflict, whose interests and whose good should have priority?' It can be stated straight away that there is one truth common to the fundamental insights of the philosophy of all times, and this is that these two questions cannot be answered independently of each other. But more of that later. The point is that reflection on these questions is what we call *philosophical* reflection.

The first thing we need to be sure about is whether we are justified in asking such questions at all, for many would deny this. It is common to come across the idea that ethical questions are meaningless because there are no answers to them or that ethical statements are not 'verifiable'. The argument goes that it is possible to derive reasonable and generally valid insights at the level of 'good for Peter's health' or 'good for Paul's tax-returns', but that this is not the case when the word 'good' is taken at an absolute level, for then pronouncements become relative to the particular culture or time in which they are made, and dependent on the social class and character of whoever is making them. It is further maintained that this position can be supported with wide-ranging empirical evidence. Reference can be made for example to cultures where human sacrifice is regarded as 'good', to societies where slavery is accepted, to the Ancient Roman law which entitled a father to do away with his own new-born child, to the contrast between Islamic culture where polygamy is acceptable and Christianity which sanctions only monogamy, and so on.

The fact that ethical codes are to a large extent culture-relative is very often cited as a reason for rejecting the possibility of moral philosophy, that is to say, the possibility of reasoned discussion about the meaning of the word 'good' in an absolute rather than a relative sense. But what this sort of argument fails to take into account is that moral philosophy does not have to disregard this fact in order to function. On the contrary, it was the very discovery of this problem which provided the impetus for rational consideration of the question as to whether there could be a generally valid idea of the good. In the fifth century B.C. the problem was already quite familiar. In Greece at that time there were any number of travel stories amongst which were to be found all sorts of weird and wonderful tales about the customs of neighbouring peoples. Yet the Greeks were not content simply to regard these customs as absurd, despicable or primitive. Some of them, the philosophers, began to look for a single standard by means of which different ethical codes and forms of life could be evaluated and compared, in the hope that it might be possible to decide, eventually, that some were better than others. They called this standard '*physis*' or Nature. Measured on this standard, for example, the Amazonian girls' practice of cutting off one breast would be inferior to the opposite practice of not doing so. This is a particularly simple and clear example. However the standard 'Nature' was by no means suitable as a means of solving all questions about the good life without further ado. For the moment, though, all we are trying to show is that the desire to find a generally valid standard for talking about a good or bad life, or good or bad actions, actually arises out of the observation that moral and ethical codes differ one from another. Therefore, reference to cultural differences does not constitute a valid argument against attempting to find such a standard.

Yet why should anyone want to establish a standard of this nature? Why should we assume that the words 'good' and 'evil', 'good' and 'bad', have a meaning which is not only absolute but also generally valid? This is not the right way to put the question. What is at issue here is not a supposition or assumption, but a certainty we all sense, so long as we do not start specifically to reflect on it. If we hear of parents cruelly mistreating a child because it accidentally wet the bed, we do not conclude that this behaviour was 'good' from the point of view of the parents because they found it satisfying, but at the same time 'bad' for the child; we quite simply condemn the parents' action because we would find it bad in an absolute sense for parents to do anything which is bad for a child. If we were to hear of a society where this sort of behaviour was customary, we would simply conclude that that particular society had bad customs. Likewise when someone acts like the Polish priest Maximilian Kolbe who volunteered to face death in a starvation cell in Auschwitz in place of a man who had a wife and children, then we do not

4

conclude that this action was good for the man and bad for the priest, or that it was in some way morally neutral from an absolute standpoint. On the contrary, we regard a man like this as someone who has preserved the honour of the human race, in spite of its besmirchment by his murderers. Surely the same feeling of admiration will be felt by Australian aborigines every bit as much as by Europeans wherever Kolbe's story is told. But we do not need to confine ourselves only to dramatic and exceptional cases. The moral outlooks of different cultures and epochs have more much in common than we often think.

We often fall victim to a kind of optical illusion. We see differences more clearly because common features are self-evident. In all cultures parents have duties towards their children, children have duties to their parents, everywhere gratitude is regarded as 'good', so too everywhere the miser is despised and the man of generous spirit held in high esteem; almost everywhere impartiality is regarded as the principal virtue of the judge and courage is regarded as the principal virtue of the warrior. The argument that here we are dealing only with trivial norms easily explained in terms of biological and social usefulness is untenable. For anyone possessing some insight into what it is to be a human being, general moral rules which apply to all human beings are bound to be trivial. And the observation that these rules are useful to the human race is just as trivial. One would hardly expect a rule to be regarded as appropriate if its adoption led to general harm. There could hardly be anything more useful to man than that which corresponds to his nature. The point though is that biological and social usefulness does not form the basis of our value judgments, and that morality, ethics and the idea of the morally good cannot be defined in such terms. We would value the action of Maximilian Kolbe even if the father whose life he saved had been killed the next day. A gesture of friendship or gratitude would still be good even if the world came to an end tomorrow. It is our experience of so many common features in the moral codes of different societies, together with our experience of the spontaneity of our own absolute value judgments of certain types of actions, which justifies the theoretical project of attempting to give an account of these general and unconditional judgments, providing, as they do, a standard of right living.

Yet it is the fact that cultural differences exist which presents us with the challenge of trying to establish a standard by which judgments can be made. The question is still whether it is possible for there to be such a standard. Up till now we have dealt only with preliminary arguments to provide a framework for further discussion. The next job is to attempt to get a more definite answer to the question. This will be done by examining two arguments which seem to be at odds with one another but have one thing in common, which is that they claim that there can be no generally valid ethical norms, that is to say, they are both forms of cultural relativism. The first thesis argues, broadly, that everyone should adhere to the moral code prevalent in his own society. The second urges that everyone should follow their inclinations and do as they please. Neither thesis stands up to rational scrutiny. Let us consider first of all the thesis that 'everyone should follow the moral code prevalent in his own society'. This idea gets caught up in three self-contradictions.

It is self-contradictory first because arguing for this position inevitably means arguing for the establishment of at least one generally valid norm; that all should follow the prevailing moral code. It could be answered that what is meant here is not a norm contained within a society but a kind of 'super-' or 'meta-norm', belonging to a quite separate category to the norms involved in moral codes. But the situation is not as simple as all that. An important aspect of a prevalent moral code may well be, for example, that one should think ill of the moral codes of other societies and that one should hold in contempt anyone adhering to them. So if we live in a cultural situation where that sort of moral code prevails, we have to hold in contempt any moral code which does not do this. The prevalent moral code of a particular society may even involve some kind of missionary zeal which requires its members to infiltrate other cultures with a view to altering their moral codes. Under these circumstances it would be impossible to follow the original rule, which was that all men should adhere to the moral code prevalent in their society. If we adhere to the moral code prevalent in our society, we are forced to try to dissuade others from adhering to their moral code. In a society like this, living according to the original rule would be impossible.

The second point is that it is not always possible to speak of *the* prevalent moral code. In our pluralistic society several different moral viewpoints co-exist and compete. For example there are some who regard abortion as a criminal act. There are others for whom it is acceptable and who will even go so far as to try to help people overcome the feelings of guilt which abortion may give rise to. So the principle that we should commit ourselves to the moral code prevalent at the time does not actually help us to decide which prevalent moral code we should actually opt for.

Third, there are societies which take as a model for moral behaviour some founding father, prophet, reformer or revolutionary, whose own conduct by no means conformed to the moral code of his own time but in fact changed it. Now of course we may consider his standards to be valid once and for all, and that no more fundamental changes are necessary, but this would be because we are convinced of the rightness of the internal content of his precepts, not just because we think that conforming is the right thing to do, for the model of moral excellence here is someone who has not conformed. So the question remains; if we are to conform in principle, to whom or what should we conform?

So much for the first thesis. It got involved in the contradictions discussed because it granted absolute status to the moral code which happened to prevail at a particular time and then went on to use this moral code to define the words 'good' and 'bad'.

By contrast the second thesis condemns every moral code adopted in practice as repressive or constrictive and urges that each individual should act according to inclination and seek happiness in which ever way he thinks fit. It would be the job of criminal justice and the police to make sure that any generally anti-social actions were so disadvantageous for persons wanting to commit them that they would see it as being in their interests not to do so. The first thesis could be regarded as authoritarian and this second thesis could be regarded as the anarchistic or individualistic version. Let us look at it more closely. At first sight it seems to have less going for it than the first thesis because it more obviously goes against the grain of our moral sensibilities. But from a theoretical point of view it is harder to refute because of the fact that it shares characteristics with the sort of thoroughgoing amoralism which recognizes no other definition of 'good' and 'evil' than 'good for X in a certain respect'. The trouble is that anyone who is genuinely unable to see a value distinction between, say, the loyalty of a mother to her child, the sacrifice of Maximilian Kolbe, the crime of his executioners, the unscrupulousness of a drug-pusher and the skill of someone speculating on the stock market is, by definition, so lacking in certain fundamental experiences and certain fundamental capacities for experience that no amount of rational argument could make up for them. As Aristotle writes, 'Anyone who says matricide is permissible is not worth arguing against, only beating.' It could also be argued that what such a person really needed was a friend to put him back on the right lines, granted of course that he was capable of friendship at all. Nonetheless, the fact that such a person might not listen to any arguments does not mean that there are no arguments against his point of view.

On closer inspection the thesis 'everyone should do as they please' turns out to be trivial anyhow. Everyone does what they want in any case. People who act in accordance with their conscience do so because that is what they want to do. People obeying particular moral codes do so because that is what they want to do. So what should we make of the proposition 'everyone should do as they please' as a normative statement in ethical theory? The idea is apparently that human beings are subject to different kinds of drives or urges and that some are to be preferred to others. This, in turn, seems to rest upon the assumption that certain drives or impulses are in some way more fundamentally 'human' or 'natural' than so-called 'moral' impulses. 'Moral impulses' are regarded as having a source which lies outside the subject and are therefore seen as a kind of internalized tyranny from which freedom should be sought. But this argument for self-determination, that is, for what is natural as opposed to what is imposed from without, inevitably leads what started out as a protest against morality, straight back into the tradition of moral philosophy. This is because the starting point for moral philosophy was the need, in view of the different sorts of customs to be found in different societies, to try to establish what actually is 'natural' to man. It was thought that the only way for a man to be free was for him to act in accordance with his nature. But what does that mean?

The argument that everyone should do what they want leads round and round in circles. This is because it fails to take into account the fact that man is not pre-determined by his instincts but is a being who has to make a conscious effort to discover the principles which lead him to act the way he does. We do not even receive language as a 'gift of nature'. We have to learn it. Unlike animals we cannot just 'be' if we are to be human; our lives are not simply automatic. We have, as people say, to 'make a life for ourselves'. We do have competing impulses and desires. The trouble with the maxim 'do as you please' is that it assumes that we know already what we want.

However it is not possible for us to get a clear idea of what it is for a will to come to be in harmony with itself without reference to the meaning of the word 'good'. This word provides the basic orientation or perspective according to which we can order all other considerations which give us reason to do one thing rather than another. Although we are not yet in a position to define this perspective we are in a position to say what it does not consist in. It cannot consist in health because at times it might actually be good for someone to be ill; nor can it consist in professional success because at times it might be good for a person to be somewhat less than successful; nor can it consist in altruism because sometimes it is good to think of oneself. The attempt to replace the word 'good' with another word, that is to say, with some other, specific viewpoint or perspective, is what G. E. Moore termed 'the naturalistic fallacy'. If 'good' really meant for example just 'healthy', then it would no longer be possible to say that health is usually something good, because all you would be saying is that health is healthy.

Right living, living the good life, means first and foremost ordering one's priorities into a correct hierarchy. The philosophers of antiquity thought they knew what the criteria for such a hierarchy would be. They thought it would be one which enabled man to live happily and in friendship with himself. This would not of course result from any old hierarchy of priorities; that is one reason why the maxim 'do what you want' does not get close enough to solving the problem of what one should want. But there is another reason why it is not enough. It is not only my inclinations which are at issue but also the inclinations of other people. That is why 'everyone should do as they please' is an ambiguous rule. It could mean either that everyone should come to terms with the inclinations of others in whatever way suits them, be this calmly and tolerantly, or violently and intolerantly. On the other hand it could mean that everyone should respect the inclinations of others. Yet such a requirement for general tolerance acts as a constraint upon what it is permissible to desire or prefer for oneself. It should be clear by now that tolerance

10

is not the obvious outcome of moral relativism, as is often maintained. It would be truer to say that the idea of tolerance has its roots in specifically moral convictions, convictions which, moreover, require some notion of universal validity. The moral relativist can always answer, 'Why should I be tolerant? My moral code permits me to be violent and intolerant.'

Some idea of the individual worth of every human being is necessary if one is to see any point in the idea that one should be tolerant. There is also the problem that the idea that one should be tolerant does nothing at all to help settle conflicts between the wishes of one person and those of another. Some wishes are simply incompatible with others. Just as there can be different sorts of wishes competing with one another at different levels within one individual, so too there can be conflicts between the wishes of different persons. There is nothing good either about always giving preference to one's own wishes or always giving preference to those of others. It is essential to take into account exactly which wishes of which person are in competition with which wishes of which other person. The only possible way of settling differences of this nature would be by means of reference to a viable, generalizable and indeed verifiable standard of comparison. The starting point of ethical relativism is the idea that agreement about such a standard is not actually possible. Yet this argument ends up proving exactly what it sets out to refute. No theoretical disputes could sensibly take place unless there were prior agreement that there is such a thing as universally applicable truth. If there were as many 'truths' as there are people, there could never be such disputes; each individual would just assert his or her own ideas until such a time as actual conflict arose. But there would still be no way this conflict could be solved by rational reflection or even by rational dispute about the standards of judgment which should be used. It could only be solved by the physical self-assertion of the strongest party who would make sure that he got his way with the minimum of fuss.

11

The fox and the hare do not argue with one another about the right way to live; they both go about their own way or one eats the other.

The fact that there are disputes about 'good' and 'evil' certainly does show that ethics is a controversial subject. But this fact proves also that ethics is not merely relative. This remains true in spite of the fact that on occasions it is hard to ascertain exactly what the good consists in and that some borderline cases are very hard to decide. It demonstrates also that some types of actions are better than others, and better in an unconditional way, not just better for a particular person or better in relation to a particular set of cultural norms. We all know that. The point of moral philosophy is to help us to get clearer about what this knowledge consists in and to help us defend it against objections raised by sophists.

Chapter two

Upbringing:
the pleasure-principle
and the reality-principle

The aim of the first chapter was to remind us of something we already knew, that there is a difference between such things as better and worse, and good and evil. It was argued that this difference is not relative to the needs of particular individuals but that it implies the possibility of making absolute value judgments independent of individual circumstances. We also know, if unreflectingly, that there is universal agreement about this difference, in spite of individual historical and cultural variations in detail. This is because it is always possible for us to compare the moral norms of different cultures with our own. As such it is even possible that we might come to regard the standards of some other cultures as being superior to those of our own.

The first thing we did was to defend this basic knowledge against certain attacks from sceptics and relativists. Before we can achieve a more precise understanding of what we actually mean when we talk of right and wrong living, of good and bad or of good and evil, there are a number of further considerations to be dealt with. This is our next task.

We are used to the idea of looking at moral questions in terms of what we 'ought' to do, that is in terms of duties and laws. But duties must be able to affect our will since we cannot act without willing to. If we ought to do something, that is tantamount to saying that we ought to want to do it.

That is why there is a way in which the statement 'I do what I want to do' is tautological. It was pointed out in chapter one that everyone does what they want to do anyhow. The question is why we should want to do anything. If you obey the doctor and give up the pleasure of eating fatty foods you do so basically because you want to stay healthy. In a more extreme case, if you hand over your wallet to a mugger you do so because you want to stay alive and not get hurt. A person totally without wants would be impervious to the requirements of duty. For someone in a pathological state of apathy the idea of 'ought' is not a meaningful one.

When philosophical reflection on ethics, that is, on the right way to live, first got going about 2,500 years ago, the first question to be asked, right at the beginning of it all, was not 'what should we do?', but 'what do we fundamentally and truly want?'. We do not want most things for their own sake but as a means to achieving something else, as the examples of the doctor and the mugger show. Every 'ought' has to be linked to a want of some kind, otherwise we would have no reason to act on it. The Greeks thought that if we could arrive at a precise understanding of the object of our basic and fundamental wants, then we would also know what we ought to do and what right living would consist of. The Greeks called this object of our most fundamental wants, the underlying reason for all our other desires and the reason for all our actions, the Good, or the highest good.

The question 'What is the highest Good?', which was central to all ethical thought in Antiquity, did not mean 'What is morally justified?' but 'What, in fact, is the ultimate goal of our striving?'. The idea was that if we knew this then we would be in a position to decide whether different moral codes were natural or unnatural and oppressive. A moral code would be natural if it helped us to achieve what we fundamentally and truly wanted, and unnatural if it failed to do this. There are two ways in which a moral code could be unnatural. On the one hand it could deliver man up to sources of control which lie outside himself or on the other hand it could leave him to the mercy of his own selfish and unreflecting whims.

Sources of control which lie outside us do actually affect what we want. A person in a position of power can make the fulfilment of our desires depend on our fulfilling his desires, although his wishes may actually be opposed to ours, as in the case of the robber who only lets us live if we hand over the money. As such we can come to adopt moral norms which are not actually in our own interests, because we only get what we actually want if we act in accordance with these norms. It is this which can lead to certain moral codes becoming 'internalized tyrannies'.

A moral code would also be unnatural though if it left us entirely to our own caprice, that is, to the kind of passing whims and moods which cause us to fail to achieve what we really want, either because these stop us from seeing things or because they result in a lack of self-control.

But should we speak in terms of one basic drive underlying all human wants, which can be used as a measure of all individual wishes and strivings and as a measure of the moral codes prevalent in particular societies? What would such a drive consist in?

The earliest answer given to this question, which is still widespread today, is that our most basic and fundamental desire, the reason why we do everything else, is the pursuit of pleasure and the avoidance of pain, or, more simply, that we want to feel good. Whatever helps us to achieve this goal is good; whatever works against it is bad. This view is termed 'hedonism', from the Greek word *hedone*, which means 'pleasure'. Hedonism was the first fruit of reflection on the basis of human conduct and as such constituted the first attempt to systematize morality. Although it is inadequate, as we shall see, we must first recognize that it does contain a discovery. This is the discovery mentioned at the beginning of the chapter, that before we can say that we 'ought' to do something, there must be a sense in which we 'want' to do it. Before I can do something which is good in itself, it also has to seem good to the person doing it, otherwise there would be no motive for doing it. There would have to be something or

15

other satisfying about the action, or else the person would simply not want to do it.

Hedonism however interprets its own discovery incorrectly. From the fact that some sense of satisfaction is inevitably present whenever we achieve something we want to achieve, it is concluded that this sense of satisfaction is the real goal of the action. Everything else we may have wanted is seen as secondary to the achievement of this goal. This assertion is groundless. Of course it makes us happy if we manage to save someone's life or show gratitude to someone who has helped us, and thereby make that person happy. But it is unrealistic to suggest that we do these things merely for the satisfaction we get out of them. Such an interpretation could only be made in retrospect by an outside observer, or as a result of the kind of reflection in which we become, as it were, spectators of our own acts of will, which is quite different from simply wanting something and doing it.

Of course not all philosophical hedonists made this mistake. Several of them, like Epicurus for example, were well aware that in general people were not concerned exclusively with the fulfilment of their desires, but with different sorts of things in life, some important, some unimportant, some good, some bad. However he thought this was symptomatic of man's alienation from himself, of a state in which unhappiness would be bound to prevail because people were failing to achieve what they wanted to achieve. So he was not saying that all men are hedonists, but recommending that it would be better if they were. He thought that we should learn that the highest good does not consist in things or in people but in the satisfaction which we find in things or in people.

There are two varieties of hedonism, positive and negative. The former is concerned primarily with the maximization of pleasure and the latter with the avoidance of pain. The former is more suited to the ruling class of a society which believes itself to be in possession of the means needed to support an increase in desire. The other variety is primarily ascetic. It maintains that desires should be kept to a minimum in order that disappointment and frustration should be kept to a minimum also. This was Epicurus' position. It is mostly associated with concern for health. In the long term good health is obviously a pre-requisite of pleasure-maximization.

In addition there is a third point to be considered which is that the degree of happiness we feel is by no means independent of the range of expectations we have. Anyone used to the satisfaction of many different sorts of needs does not in the long term necessarily experience a greater quantity of pleasure than someone whose needs are more modest. The rich man's needs may be harder to achieve and take more time to organize, time being the one thing he does not possess in large measure. Also his pleasures may be more fragile. So, from Epicurus' point of view, keeping one's desires to a minimum is in fact a reasonable thing to do.

Lastly, Epicurus thought that virtues like goodwill, friendship, and generosity also belonged to the good life, these qualities being a source of happiness to anyone possessing them. Jesus' saying, 'It is more blessed to give than to receive' can be defended on hedonistic grounds. Hedonism contains important insights central to the art of living, but these insights are spoilt, as we shall see, because concentrating on personal attainment of pleasure in fact stands in the way of true happiness.

Before dealing with this it is worth pointing out that even if we do accept that human striving aims first and foremost at the increase of pleasure, still, very early in man's development, another sort of drive develops alongside it, the drive for self-preservation. In the case of animals there is a direct link between the instinct to preserve self and species and the drive towards the increase of pleasure and the avoidance of pain. In natural environmental conditions an animal will enjoy eating exactly that food which is most likely to guarantee its survival. There is no need for the animal even to think about the survival of the species; this is taken care of by its sex drive. But although man is equipped with a sex drive, as well as the capacity to feel hunger and thirst, explicit reflection about these drives and what it is to satisfy them can have the effect of detaching them from their natural purpose, which is the survival and the preservation of the species. The world in which we live is not a fixed environment where everything is determined in advance by instinct but a place where there are endless possibilities for satisfaction and of course endless threats – for not all our wishes can be satisfied with impunity.

It is for reasons such as these that Sigmund Freud used the terms pleasure-principle and reality-principle in his description of the early development of children. He saw the child as equipped initially with nothing more than an indeterminate libido, a desire for pleasure, bodily contact and union. Soon though the child experiences reality as something which harshly, automatically and unconditionally stands in opposition to this drive. Reality will not adapt itself to us; we have to adapt ourselves to reality. We have to forego some of our desires in order to be able to satisfy others, indeed, in order to be able to survive at all. Freud thought that the reality-principle was the origin of reason. In some cloud-cuckoo-land, where every wish could immediately and effortlessly be fulfilled, and in which we did not have to pay heed to any considerations outside ourselves, there would be no need for reason or anything like it to develop. Thus Freud saw the whole of human life in terms of a compromise, a compromise which was essential to our survival – a compromise between what we actually want, that is to say the unlimited gratification of our libido, and adaptation to the reality which stands in the way of this. Man is seen as an inhibited hedonist. Freud saw this as the root of all neuroses, and also of all the higher achievements of culture, which, in his view, arose out of the so-called sublimation of the primary drives.

Freud brought to light phenomena which until then had remained hidden. But was his interpretation correct? An

18

answer is provided by the following thought-experiment. Let us imagine a man strapped to a table in an operating theatre. He is under anaesthetic and there are electrodes attached to his scalp. Precisely measured electrical impulses are transmitted through these wires to certain brain-centres which induce a permanent state of euphoria. The person's beatific expression reflects his state. The doctor who is carrying out the experiment explains to us that the man will remain in this condition for at least another ten years. When at last it is no longer possible to prolong it, the machine will be switched off and he will immediately die without feeling any pain. The doctor offers the same to us. The question is, who amongst us would be prepared to allow him- or herself to be transported into this kind of bliss?

The conclusion we have to draw from our unwillingness to accept such an offer is that what we most truly and most fundamentally want is not the maximization of pleasure; the man on the table obviously enjoys the most extreme feelings of pleasure, and yet we do not want to change places with him. We would rather continue to lead our humdrum lives. The reason we do not want to change places with him is that he is in a situation which is outside real life, outside reality. He does not realize this; for all we know his dreams may contain the most delightful people. Yet we prefer more ordinary people who are correspondingly more real. It is not true at all that we have to see reality's primary function as being to stand in our way and oppose us, nor is it something that we are forced, against our will, to conform to, for we have to admit that we would not give it up at any price. Within reality, pleasure and pain are inextricably bound together. Pain, so long as it is not excessive, has an important function. It shows us the dangers in life, and as such serves the end of self-preservation. Indeed it is true to say that the drive for self-preservation constrains the pleasure-drive, but not in a way which constitutes only an empty compromise, for it should be clear by now that increase of pleasure is not the main thing which we fundamentally and most truly desire; increase of pleasure is no more than a desirable by-product. On the other hand, the experience of reality, far from representing a barrier to our fulfilment in life, in fact turns out to be the real content of our life. The fact that our very survival is always at stake, alongside the fact that our lives are certain to end in death, is, strange though it may seem, the one thing which makes it possible for us to make sense of our lives.

Let us now try another thought-experiment. Imagine we have just found out that we will never die. This is not to say that we will enter a higher form of existence after death, in the way that Christianity teaches us, but that we will continue to live forever just as we are now, without pain and without growing old. If the full implications of this are grasped, it becomes clear that the situation would be catastrophic. Quite a few of us would not mind living for two hundred years, but to live endlessly would mean that every moment, every joy, every human encounter would pale into insignificance. Everything which we do now we may just as well do tomorrow or the next day. Nothing would matter to us. The preciousness of each moment consists precisely in the fact that never again in one's life will it return. In endless life there would be nothing precious. This, then, results in the paradoxical situation that we need the anxiety which arises out of the threat of extinction in order to be able to lead fulfilled lives.

So self-preservation is not, any more than increase in pleasure, the purpose of life. If it were, we would want to be able to live endlessly. But we do not want this, and we do not want self-preservation at any price any more than we want increase in pleasure at any price. It is possible to sacrifice one's life for another person. It is possible for a man, as Brecht says 'to fear his wretched life more than death'. Alongside hedonistic moral systems, and as a reaction against them, there have been, in the history of ethics, moral systems based on the idea of self-preservation, systems of norms where everything is subordinated to the central idea of self-preservation, be this the preservation of the individual or of a whole social system.

What this point of view fails to take into account is *what* actually is being preserved. It sacrifices consideration of what kind of life is worth living to consideration of how life is best to be preserved. It is for this reason that in this sort of moral system we find no attempt to define *what* the word 'good' means. The two points of view, consideration of what it is to lead a fulfilled life and consideration of how life is best preserved, should not be seen as separate, not even in the realm of politics. Freedom and well-being would probably soon come to an end in a society which defines its citizens' rights to liberty and private gratification exclusively in terms of self-preservation and security. On the other hand, a political system geared to guarantee freedom, even to the extent that the continued existence of that society were sub-ordinated to this end, would place in jeopardy the very thing it was aiming to preserve, and which might have made the system worth preserving. So the good life can be destroyed, one might say, by deviations either to the left or to the right.

In fact no system can survive unless it is capable of undergoing certain types of change and adapting to the environment. If a system is too rigid it will break down; if it takes adaptation and change too far it will lose its identity and fail to survive also, since it will no longer count as the same system. Any fixation with self-preservation, be this through rigid conservatism or over-flexibility, will stand in the way of successful living. The relationship between survival and fulfilment if of a dialectical nature. Whether a person is more strongly inclined one way or the other depends on his character, on whether he is more worried about missing out on something or on losing it altogether. The political left and right can, as said, be categorized in terms of these two tendencies, the pleasure-principle and the reality-principle, the principle of fulfilment and the principle of preservation.

In the 1960s, Herbert Marcuse, one of the intellectual gurus of the left, defended the view that the dominion of the reality-principle, which Freud had thought would always be unavoidable, could be relaxed in a consumer society where there was an abundance of material goods. This sort of society seemed then to be within reach. 'Power to fantasy!' was the slogan to be found on the walls of the Sorbonne in 1968. This was very much in line with the ideas which Herbert Marcuse was putting forward. To those committed to this hope, the oil crisis and everything that followed must have been extremely disillusioning. But disillusionment is always a good thing, because having illusions is always bad. Reality will only appear hostile to a person who sees man as a being whose ultimate and most fundamental aim is the maximization of subjective pleasure. But a person who understands that we actually want reality, that we can only come to terms with ourselves if we experience and respond actively to reality, will see things differently. Such a person will understand that the good is linked to experiencing reality and dealing fairly with it.

Although the title of this chapter is 'Upbringing: the pleasure-principle and the reality-principle', the word 'upbringing' has not yet been mentioned. Yet all the time this has been the real subject of discussion. The starting point for all ethics, all deliberate and conscious questioning about the good life, is the process by which the child is carefully and purposefully led forth out of the constraints of its own subjective world of feelings into reality, the real world which exists, as it is, in a way which does not depend on us. Rousseau once recommended that if a child being carried by its mother reaches out its hand for an apple, the mother should not fetch the apple for the child but carry the child to the apple. In this way the child would learn that things cannot simply be ordered about but that we have to move also. Thus Matthias Claudius wrote to his son Johannes: 'The truth, my dear son, does not accommodate itself to us, we have to accommodate ourselves to it.' The important thing to realize is that this is not *unfortunately* the case, but *fortunately* so. It is only in the context of a reality which at times stands in opposition to us that we can develop our powers. Any deeper sense of joy in life depends on the development both of our strengths and our capacities. The task of anyone entrusted with the care of a child is to help the child come to terms with reality, both the self-sufficiency of reality and its tendency to stand in opposition to us. In general the mother is the first self-sufficient reality a child comes across. The result of this is that the child initially experiences reality as something kind and helpful. The legacy of this experience, what psychologists call 'primitive trust', is the most significant gift a good upbringing can bestow. A person who is able to fall back on a memory of what it is like for there to be harmony in the world will be able to deal more easily with a world in which there is discord.

Chapter three

Education: self-interest and a sense of values

What do we fundamentally and truly want? That was the question which we considered in the last chapter, and which led us into the mainstream of investigations in the classical tradition of philosophy. We discussed hedonism, the solution which immediately presents itself when a whole ethical system loses for the first time its immediate and self-evident validity. Hedonism has it that what we truly and fundamentally want is increase of pleasure or comfort. The limitations of this view were discussed and it was seen that in general we want something else too, which is our own survival. Freud said that the pleasure-principle is constrained by the reality-principle; he saw man as an inhibited hedonist, forced to adapt, whether he likes it or not, to a hostile reality, for the sake of his own survival. But this view, as we saw, does not do justice to the facts. This is because we actually *want* reality; provided we are not ill or addicted to drugs, we do not want any illusory euphoria, but happiness based on contact with reality.

We need now to proceed one step further in our reflections about what constitutes the good life. In reality the pursuit of pleasure and self-preservation are abstract concepts which, whether we consider them together or in isolation, do not adequately describe what most fundamentally concerns us.

In one of Plato's dialogues Socrates replies to someone who is arguing that increase of pleasure is the one goal worth striving for. His reply is that in that case the happiest man in the world would be someone who always has an itch and is always able to scratch it. His opponent bemoans his lack of taste. Surely there are higher forms of pleasure than scratching oneself. But how are we to distinguish higher forms of pleasure from lower ones?

The distinction is present in everyday language. We do not usually talk of higher pleasures in terms of 'pleasure' at all; instead we use other words like 'joy'. The curious thing is that we can find ourselves in a depressed mental state at the very same time that we are enjoying physical pleasure; also we can experience intense joy despite being in physical pain, provided of course that the pain is not so intense that it absorbs all our attention. Furthermore there can be no doubt as to which of the two states is preferable; for the depressed person experiences no pleasure; but the person who rejoices, rejoices. There is no sense in asking what anyone gets out of joy. You do not get anything out of joy, but when we get something out of something else, that is joy. You cannot get more out of anything than joy. There is no accident in the fact that we can talk of feeling joy both *at* and *about* something. Feelings of pleasure are caused by something, but joy has an *object* or a *content*. When it comes down to it there are as many different types of joy as there are possible objects of joy. The joy one might feel listening to the Rolling Stones is different from the joy brought about by listening to the Beatles; the joy one might feel listening to Beethoven's *Hammerklavier Sonata* is different to the joy of listening to the *Waldstein;* the joy felt in the presence of one friend will be different from the joy felt in the presence of another, and so on.

We call contents or objects of feeling 'values'. The value content of reality is revealed to us in acts of joy and sorrow, admiration and disdain, love and hate, hope and fear. There is a paradox in the fact that anyone who makes the pursuit of pleasure and subjective well-being his purpose in life and the goal of his actions will cut himself off from the experience of the deeper kind of well-being, which we call joy. We can only experience this if we are capable of perceiving the values inherent in reality in all their richness and if we are capable of looking beyond ourselves and rejoicing *at* or *about* things just as they are.

Such values are not all accessible to us at first. They are revealed only gradually and only to the extent that we learn to regard our own interests in an objective way. One has to *learn* how to listen to good music in such a way so one can enjoy it fully; one has to *learn* how to read a text attentively, and to understand other people; the same is even true of telling the difference between different wines, for the pleasures of the wine connoisseur, of which the uninitiated can have no concept, presuppose the process of educating the palate.

Education is the name we give to the process whereby a human being is led out of the animal preoccupation with self to a state where he is able to be objective about his own interests and differentiate between them, in such a way that his capacity to experience joy and pain is increased. It is often said nowadays that the job of education is to teach young people how to stand up for their own interests. Yet there is a much more fundamental task which is to teach people how to *have* interests, that is to say, how to be interested in something. If all a person has learnt is how to stand up for his own interests, but is interested in nothing apart from himself, there is no way that person can be happy. Therefore education, in the sense that it develops interests of an objective nature, and leads to an appreciation of the value content of reality, is an essential element of successful living.

It is part of the nature of our perception of values, that we do not perceive individual values in isolation, but in the overall context of our likes and dislikes. If a person adopts certain values there comes into being for him a kind of objective hierarchy of values. To a person who has no particular attachment either to Bach or to Telemann, it may well seem arbitrary which of the two composers is most highly rated. But to someone with any real knowledge of them both such a thought would be impossible. Even someone who personally had a particular preference for Telemann would still regard Bach as the greater of the two.

This sort of hierarchy becomes really important when dealing with different categories of values. One might take for example the value of courage involved in holding fast to a principle of justice compared with the value of the capacity to enjoy pleasure. There can be no doubt but that this latter is valuable. The point though is that no-one who had any appreciation of the two would regard them as being entirely of equal value. That would be a contradiction. A courageous person is by definition someone who prefers to hold fast to justice than to enjoy pleasure undisturbed. If pleasure were exactly as valuable as holding fast to what is just, then it would quite simply be unreasonable to be courageous, and courage itself would be valueless. Courage has to be seen either as having no value at all, or as having a higher value than pleasure. It is in the nature of higher values that they are either perceived as being of a higher order, or not perceived at all. The education of a person's sense of values, his sense of a hierarchy of values, and his ability to distinguish what is important from what is not important, is necessary for the success of each individual's life, and it is also a prerequisite of his ability to communicate with others.

Individual life consists of a series of temporal states. If a human life is to be successful, these states should not be disconnected, as they are for the schizophrenic; happiness comes from being reconciled with oneself. This presupposes that there must be some continuity in our acts of will. We have to be able to start something one day in the knowledge that, provided nothing unforeseen intervenes, we will be able to continue with it the next. Also, if we think something is good one day, we should at least be able to see why we thought so the day after. If our states and our actions are nothing more than the function of random external stimuli and interior moods which are not founded on some insight into an objective hierarchy of values, then we lack the foundation on which to build a state of wholeness and harmony with ourselves. In this sort of state there can be no way of living in harmony with others either. If subjective interests are seen merely in terms of egoism, that is, if they are seen as arising purely and simply out of the nature of the individuals in question, then it becomes quite impossible to reconcile them. If each individual stubbornly insists that he wants one thing or another and there are no common standards by means of which a hierarchy of values can be established to give an order of priority in terms of relative worth and urgency, then it will not be possible to reconcile conflicting interests. Dialogue, discussion and debate, in spite of what is generally thought nowadays, would all be useless in trying to bridge the gap. This would be because those taking part in such discussions would be incapable of ordering and comparing interests in terms of objective viewpoints. Just like small children they would only ever say, 'But I want that!'

In reality though, day in and day out, countless numbers of agreements do take place, and this is because of the fact that those involved share certain common insights into the relative merits and importance of the interests under discussion; also they do not consider just *whose* interests are at stake, but fortunately also *which* interests. If, for example, the interests of smokers and non-smokers come into conflict, and it is decided to create a no-smoking area, this would not be because the non-smokers were better people (the smokers would be right to dispute this), but because the values to which the non-smokers appeal have priority over the enjoyment of smoking. There is no reason why smokers should not submit themselves to such a judgment, however inconvenient it may be to them, for the simple reason, that they can see the point of it.

Anyone capable of acting in accordance with some understanding of values, despite the fact that this may stand in the way of his immediate gratification, is capable of acting in what we would call a moral way. The ability to acquire moral insights grows in proportion to one's

28

readiness to act in accordance with them. Conversely it diminishes where this readiness is lacking. Discussion and teaching are not necessarily the best ways of gaining insights into values compared with experience and practice. Anyone going to an exhibition of modern art for the first time will probably make hasty and generalizing judgments about the exhibition, and only discover ways of categorizing and evaluating individual works when he has learnt the language of this sort of art, that is to say, when he has become familiar with a lot of examples. Of course there are going to be disputes about how works should be categorized and evaluated, even amongst those who are educated to do this, but these disputes are not so fundamental.

In literary criticism nowadays there is a tendency quite simply to put questions of value to one side, and to deal with, say, Shakespeare's *King Lear,* as though it were on a par with a cheap and ephemeral novel. This may be justified if certain specialized, formal questions involving both texts are being looked into, like for example linguistic questions, questions about grammatical structure, or the statistical frequency of certain words. Here it matters little whether or not the person doing the research is educated, in the broader sense, or not. Yet when it comes to choosing texts for study in schools or one's own private reading, then standards of value are very important. Reading is not there to serve the purposes of literary criticism, but *vice versa.* Writers and poets do not write for the sake of literary criticism but for the reader. It is a mistake to maintain that there are no criteria by means of which a hierarchy can be established. There is one very precise criterion, and that is the intensity of enjoyment associated with, for example, reading certain books. Some people may well not enjoy reading Shakespeare at all and enjoy only detective thrillers. These people would no more be able to take part in the discussion than someone who never experienced any pleasure reading a detective novel. But someone capable of enjoying both detective thrillers and Shakespeare must have experience of the fact that one brings enjoyment of a greater intensity, depth, duration and durability than the other, although this enjoyment may demand more of the reader, and be less obviously and immediately accessible.

The obtrusiveness of values is almost always in inverse proportion to their degree of elevation. This is why it requires greater self-discipline to be able even to grasp the significance of higher values, that is, those which bring most joy. They demand greater attentiveness. Attentiveness though only arises out of the self. It is a form of self-motivated activity; and it is true to say that joys arising from within, self-motivated joys, are deeper and longer lasting. Watching television requires only a minimum of self-motivation. It is interesting that certain complex statistical investigations came up with the result that people who watch a lot of television are less likely, when discussing their feelings about life, to communicate a sense of joy than people who are more inclined to read books.

There are two ways in which our sense of values can be obscured. At first sight they seem quite opposite. The first is dullness of spirit and the second is the blindness of passion. In the Old Testament there is an example of dullness of spirit giving rise to insensitivity to values in the story of Esau, who sells his birthright to Jacob for lentil soup. Jacob, egged on by his mother, is clever enough to exploit the hungry Esau's obtuseness, and his partiality to lentil soup, just at the right moment. Only much later does Esau discover how he was taken in. At the time the lentil soup seemed real and worthwhile; his birthright was some vague and abstract idea of greatness wished upon him. An obtuse person perceives no hierarchy of values.

A person blinded by passion fails to perceive values in a different way. Let us take another biblical example. King David, by no means an obtuse person, was so overwhelmed by his passion for Bathsheba, that he sent her husband to war in a place where he was sure to die. His passion for Bathsheba made him blind to the baseness of acting in such a way. In one way passion helps us to see, it opens our eyes to one particular quality, in this example to the beauty of a woman. This is why a life without passion is not actually a good life. There is something seriously lacking in someone unable to get angry about injustice. Passion reveals to us both the presence and absence of value, but at the same time it distorts the sense of proportion with which each value has to be seen. That is why a person acting in the throes of passion is not acting for the sake of the value in question, but egotistically; he obstinately insists on imposing his own view on the situation, rather than letting the situation speak for itself. There is a line in a hit record 'Can love be a sin?' Of course it cannot. Love, which reveals to us a person's worth or beauty, is something which comes over us from without. But Bathsheba's beauty was known to her husband also, and the reason why Uriah was killed was not that Bathsheba was beautiful, but because the King was of the opinion that *he* should have her and not Uriah. He saw this as being more important than Uriah's life. Bathsheba's beauty was not the actual cause. In this case the appeal to passion does not provide an excuse. Such an appeal would depend on the idea that in certain cases one can be incapable of seeing the implications of one's actions, that is to say, that one can be blind to all the various implications of one's actions but one. Yet this is not a genuine blindness. Man is not an animal. He can pretend to be blind and act as though he were unable to see. But he is responsible for his inability to see, both morally and, in our judiciary systems, legally.

Passions may well reveal values, but not their hierarchical order. That is why people are advised not to act on impulse when angry. Anger can be just, and it can be necessary, shocking us out of a state of obtuseness and causing us to face up to injustice. But anger does not make clear to us what we should actually do. That is why it can lead to new injustices, because it does not at the same time make clear the proportions in which a situation should be seen. Action is always complex and nearly always has manifold consequences. The same is true for sympathy. Sympathy helps us to see another's sorrow, but it does not make clear what should actually be done. It is possible, when acting out of sympathy, to do something quite irrational, something which may in fact do no good at all to the person for whom one feels sympathy.

There is another point too. Passions come and go, but values, often the very values revealed to us through passion, are of a lasting nature. If we act only out of passion, we will not be dealing fairly with reality. Feelings of anger may well evaporate, but it might still remain necessary to fight year after year against a particular injustice, by which time the passionate feeling of anger which first made us aware of the situation could well have turned into a calm, deep-seated sense of certainty. If we are only prepared to help people in need when actually feeling the emotion of sympathy, we will soon stop helping anyone at all; the media so overwhelm us with images of misery, that our capacity for feeling sympathy is soon exhausted. What really matters is whether or not our awareness of the need to help can outlast the feelings of sympathy which move us. The same is true of love. The very passion which causes crime to be committed for love, may also quickly put paid to that love. A man might, for example, kill his wife because he loves another woman. Then he might kill her too for love of a third. The link between love and faithfulness arises out of the fact that what, to begin with, was no more than passion, gradually takes over that person in a deeper way, so that that person's freedom is no longer restricted, but actually engaged. The relationship loses the character of a chance event, and the couple no longer feel the need to wait and see if maybe their love will simply disappear in the same mysterious way that it came upon them. They know this will not happen, because they do not want it to happen; their love has embraced their free will or, perhaps better, their free will has embraced their love. All passion can ever do is to bring us into a new relationship with a value, but it cannot tell us what an appropriate, free response to it should be.

Chapter four

Justice: myself and others

There are three main arguments against the idea that a sense of values is of fundamental significance for the living of a successful life. The first argument is that appealing to insights about values is not in fact likely to reduce conflict or bring about consensus. So if a person claims to possess some special insight into values which he is, however, unable to communicate, the reaction to him is very likely to involve conflict. The counter-argument to this is that any decision to judge ethical codes solely or predominantly in terms of conflict-reduction itself arises out of a value judgment, a value judgment which, moreover, once articulated, will not necessarily be all that helpful. Bach, Bartók and Alban Berg wrote wonderful music, music which it would be a tragedy ever to lose, and this would be true even if only a minority of people recognized the fact. It is also the case that only a minority of people recognize the value and significance of quantum physics. Insights into values can indeed bring about conflict. At the same time though these value judgments are, as previously argued, the essential condition for the overcoming of conflict. If different interests simply clash, and there is no possibility of getting them into some kind of order of priority, then there is no possibility of agreement.

The second argument is that anything we say about values is bound to be, to a certain extent, dogmatic or apodeictic, and that in order to be more scientifically responsible we should limit ourselves to a hypothetical approach. As such we would have to regard our value judgments as hypotheses open to revision at any time in the light of experience. The counter-argument to this comes from asking what learning from experience really means. It seems to mean the process of learning that one particular way of achieving an aim is more appropriate than another way. Yet this fails to take into account the question of whether or not the aim was worth achieving in the first place. You can learn what is most likely to enhance your chances of survival, your ability to communicate, bring you pleasure and so on, but this sort of learning always presupposes a value judgment about the worthwhileness of the goal. If you are not interested in survival, communication, pleasure or whatever, if you have no notion of the significance or value of anything, neither will you will be able to learn anything. That is why a value judgment is not a hypothesis but a pre-requisite without which hypotheses cannot be formed. There is no conceivable higher authority by means of which our insights about such values could come to be corrected and replaced by new insights. There is only one source of authority, but we only discover what that is when the process of re-evaluation has already been brought about. This source of authority is our newer and deeper insight into values. This happens spontaneously, not in the form of a hypothesis but as something which is self-evident. New insights are not superior because they undermine previous insights, but because they assign to them a new place in a more comprehensive scale of values.

The third argument against the idea of a sense of values is that all we are really dealing with are questions about language or linguistic analysis. The idea is that when we talk about values we have at our disposal only a certain vocabulary and that this vocabulary limits what we can say. I do not see any real problem here. There is no point in doing conceptual analysis on words unless we assume in advance that they actually mean something. In fact language does provide for us the means by which we can come to appreciate different qualities. Without certain words for different types of taste we would have difficulty telling the difference between different tastes. Languages which differentiate particularly well between different qualities actually make it possible for us to experience such qualities in a more discriminating way. There is of course more to the experience of quality than the correct usage of appropriate expressions. There is no doubt that the wine connoisseur's ability to distinguish different types of taste is closely connected with the vocabulary which he has at his disposal, the vocabulary which is used during the process of the cultivation of the palate. But the enjoyment itself is not the same thing as just using vocabulary. The same is true for all expressions of value and especially the word 'good'. The only way one can ultimately tell if someone understands the meaning of such a word, is by looking at the way it acts as a motivating factor in that person's dealings in the world. This is the idea behind Socrates' view that no one really knows what the word 'good' means, unless their actions are affected by the knowledge.

Right living, as we saw in the previous chapters, means dealing fairly with reality. In other words, we should be objective about our own interests and allow them to be formed by the value content of reality. Education, as we saw, should make us capable of freeing ourselves from the domination of the stimulus of the moment, and enable us to do what we really want to do. We should learn to live our own lives rather than having them lived for us. The object of education should be to disclose the value content of reality and develop a diversity of objective interests. Only then, by being objective about our interests and about our wishes, in a way which implies that we should acknowledge universal standards, will we be able to compare these interests with one another, and only then will it be possible for us to come to terms with competing interests, both those within ourselves and those involving other people.

Yet there is another aspect of right and successful living, which arises out of the fact that the reality with which we must deal fairly consists principally of other human beings. It is not possible to be a human being without others. Language, thought, and feeling only develop as a result of communication. The wealth of reality is only revealed through language, which binds us to others. We only even learn to walk through imitation. It is not possible to live without making one's behaviour and actions at least to some extent meaningful to others, and meaningful not just in a theoretical way, but also in a way which can be approved of and justified, especially when we are confronted with those who are affected by the consequences of our actions. Our readiness to submit our actions to a common standard of justification of this nature is what we call 'justice'.

It is possible to talk in terms of 'just' conditions, 'just' distribution of goods and so on, but in the first place justice is a virtue, that is to say, it has to do with the way people think and act. Justice can be demanded of any person at any time and with respect to any other person. Justice requires nothing less than that we should see our own sympathies, wishes, preferences, and interests as relative. If our actions affect the interests of others we cannot justify them simply by saying that they are in our interests. Our own interests may well at times have priority over those of others, however this is not because they are our interests but because of reasons inherent in the nature of the interests themselves. This means that if these interests were those of another person, then they would have to be given priority. A just person is one who judges conflicts of interests in terms of *which* interests are at stake and who is prepared to disregard the question of *whose* interests are at stake. Since, in cases of doubt, we are always tempted to give priority to our own interests and to grant privileges to ourselves, part of what justice means is that, when such cases arise, we should be ready to submit ourselves to a higher and impartial authority. That is why justice implies a readiness to submit oneself to the laws of the land and a public judiciary.

The phenomenon which lies at the heart of all systems of justice is the distribution of scarce goods and claims made upon them. The distribution of goods available in abundance is not subject to the principles of justice. The peculiar thing about Karl Marx's vision of the future is that it is not concerned with justice, but with setting up a situation where there is no more need for justice, a situation where there is abundance and everyone can just help themselves without there being any need to pay. The production of goods in this state of abundance should take up so little time that there would be no need for the criteria of justice even in the distribution of work time. This situation would be called 'communism' and in it the principle 'to each according to his needs' would hold sway.

According to Marx, progress towards this state would be dictated by the degree of efficiency which is achievable. In the meantime the only valid standard would have to be that of the principle 'from each according to his abilities, to each according to his achievement'. Before we can consider this principle, which we can call the 'principle of achievement', in relationship to justice, we need to look more closely at what we understand by justice. Justice is the recognition of a fundamental symmetry in human relationships, particularly with regard to the distribution of scarce goods. This symmetry does not consist in simple equality for all concerned, but in the recognition that asymmetries need to be justified. This justification would have to be such that anyone prepared to think in terms of justice would agree to accept the asymmetry in question. If a person is discriminated against in a way which he cannot accept as being just, and which is not in fact justifiable, for example because he is Jewish or black or the son of someone who owns a large amount of real estate, then the fundamental symmetry is infringed in a way which cannot be justified. Justice, as said, does not mean that everyone should get the same thing or achieve the same as everyone else; it means that the criteria used to decide how to distribute responsibilities and recompenses, whatever these may be, should not be drawn up in advance in such a way as to favour particular persons or groups of persons, nor, when put into practice, should they be manipulated in such a way as to favour or disadvantage any particular persons. That is why the Goddess of Justice is represented as wearing a blindfold. Justice always implies impartiality.

This is not to say that we have to be impartial at all times and in all places, because not all our actions are subject to the principles of justice. Aristotle considered two sorts of human relationship to be subject to the requirements of justice: the exchange of goods, and the distribution of responsibilities and recompense through authority.

He thought that as far as the exchange of goods was concerned, attention had constantly to be paid to the equality of value of the goods being exchanged, that is, on the price being fair. The trouble is though that price depends to a large extent on what those involved in the exchange consider the value of the goods in question to be, and this in turn depends, amongst other things, on the relative scarcity of those goods. The market price of goods follows the laws of supply and demand. At an auction one might wonder how it could be unjust to let the highest bidder have something at a price he is prepared to pay. The question of justice in exchange is seen nowadays from a slightly different point of view. We are more concerned with why someone might be prepared to pay an exorbitant price for something. If we hear of someone prepared to give up all their wealth for a glass of water we wonder if this was out of love for antique glass or because the person was dying of thirst in a desert. In the second case there is a fundamental asymmetry between the two parties, and to demand the highest price in such a situation would be a blatant injustice. Such behaviour would be seen as profiteering. Injustice lies either in exploiting another's need, that is, exploiting a dominant position in the market, in a way which makes it possible to ask any price, or else it lies in the exploitation of the ignorance of the buyer, or the seller. That is why state systems of justice are required to act against such asymmetries. Given this, a private individual would only need to possess the virtue of justice relevant to the exchange of goods if circumstances arose which were asymmetrical in a way which made it possible for him to exercise power in order to prejudice an act of exchange in his own favour.

Justice is the virtue of those in positions of power, the virtue of the strong. The weak do not need to be virtuous to be interested in symmetry. They have to be interested if they are to improve their lot. Yet they are unable to bring about a situation of symmetry, precisely because they are weak. In a situation where there is equality, as in a perfect free market economy, it would be perfectly just for everyone to take whatever they could get. However it is the privilege of the powerful to be able to apply standards other than those which happen to be to their advantage. That is to say that they can choose to share. If a person has a Stradivarius violin which he wishes to sell by auction, but is not so poor that he absolutely has to sell it to the highest bidder, then he is in a privileged position. Under these circumstances it would be just for him to sell it not to a rich collector, but to an excellent violinist, who can afford to pay perhaps only half as much, but who would be able to make better use of it.

Justice is primarily a way of deciding how scarce goods should be distributed in the context of institutions already in existence. These institutions are not the direct product of justice. No one is under a prior obligation to place their trust in another person. But once a promise has been made, the person to whom the promise was made has every right to expect it to be kept. A country is not accountable to foreigners for the requirements and standards which it takes as a basis of qualification for citizenship, but every citizen has the right to demand that his citizenship should not be taken away unless this can be justified on legal grounds or without some guilt on his part. Also of course, every person has certain fundamental obligations to act in a just way towards all other human beings simply because they belong to the human race.

In previous centuries the unity which we call 'the human race' was seen only as an abstract unity, based on the fact that its members were bound together by nothing more than their similarity to one another. In the modern world though it has for a long time been the case that there have been interconnections between different groups of people in the world, particularly economic interconnections. If these interconnections were of a reasonably symmetrical nature there would be no problem of justice. But since there are real positions of power within this system, particularly with regard to the way the world market is dominated by industrialized and oil-exporting countries, it is legitimate to call on the possessors of power to exercise justice. This is because they are more than just one party to an exchange, they are distributors, and as such it is necessary to require them to take into account the principles of distributive justice.

Yet that is not all. Although there are always situations where power can be wielded and where therefore it is legitimate to appeal to the virtue of justice, it should be remembered that this virtue, by its very nature, militates towards the creation of a situation where justice will no longer be necessary; for it is contrary to the fundamental requirement of symmetry in relationships made by justice that some people should be entirely at the mercy of others and that they should depend on these people acting justly. That is why control of power and the distribution of sources of power are part and parcel of our idea of a situation where justice prevails. It is also why a person, or a group of persons, in a position of power can only be regarded as just if they are ready to accept that their powers should be limited by legal institutions.

If we try to get at a more precise answer to the question of what distributive justice consists in, the answer we get seems, at first, to be very formal. That is why it is so often said, especially by those belonging to the neo-liberal school of thought, that there is no such thing as distributive justice. The argument goes that, from any point of view within a particular society, there are so many different criteria which could in theory be used to establish a framework for distribution, that conflict is bound to arise. The most important thing then would be for conflict to be channelled through state juridicial institutions and for various possible solutions to different conflicts to be kept open. This, they say, contrasts with the situation in totalitarian states where revision of the criteria for distributive justice is difficult. In such societies, the argument goes, the privileges of a particular class, once established, are guaranteed in an unacceptable way. The trouble is though that this criticism of the inflexibility of privilege, together with the demand for free discussion of questions of distribution, shows that, although this school of thought may claim that there is no such thing as justice, in reality its adherents regard certain specific solutions to the problem of distribution to be unjust; for example solutions which rely on the exploitation of political weakness and the oppression of a particular class of underprivileged people. Also, when they say that distribution necessarily involves conflict, there is the question of what form this conflict should take. It would not take the form of one person saying 'I want this much' and another person saying 'But I want this much too'. Both try to *justify* their position. They put forward relevant points of view. They talk in terms of just demands and so on. In other words, they talk about justice. Conflict is in fact an important means of discovering what actually is just.

The first thing that happens in court cases is that the lawyers of both parties put forward their idea of what the correct judgment should be. They do this in a one-sided way and from a one-sided point of view. Yet it is as a result of this one-sidedness that the judge, eventually, gets a genuine overview of the case and can attempt to weigh up the different points of view impartially, so as to be able to make a fair judgment. But still the question remains as to what the relevant criteria for making judgments about distribution actually are. Let us first consider two extreme answers. The first is that there is only *one* relevant point of view, that of the person who is best able to carry out his purpose, that is to say, the idea that 'might is right'. The second answer is that one can choose at will between different criteria, each being valid in its own way. In that case justice would consist only in the impartial application of whichever standard happens to have been impartially chosen.

Let us consider first the idea of the right of the strongest. This idea had already been formulated both theoretically and practically in Athens in the fifth century B.C. The sophists of the day taught that justice consisted in the strong doing what benefited them. In response Plato asked if justice actually *is* what benefits the strong, or what the strong *think* benefits them. He went on to consider the problem of what actually benefits anyone. Before this question can be answered it is necessary to know what a person actually is. The strong cannot eat much more than it takes to fill them. It might well be that what benefits the strong most of all, from the point of view of their own humanity, is to deal fairly with reality, to see the value-content of reality and to learn how to love. In that case the right of the strong could well be the right, and even more importantly, the ability, which the weak do not possess to the same extent, to be detached about their own interests, in other words, to be just. Justice is the virtue of the powerful. It is true of every herd or pack of animals that the strong use their strength to secure their own authority. But they use their authority to protect the weaker members of the pack or herd and to defend their interests against a hostile environment. Likewise in human society it is inevitable that the strong will hold power. If the strong had not been lucky enough to be born in the right place and at the right time, to be clever, more skilled, more articulate and so on, they would not have been able to achieve their positions of power. To this extent, talking about the right of the strong is trivial. The only question is what the strong, who have proven their strength by the fact that they are in positions of power, should actually do with that power, whether they should act in a way which conforms to an objective hierarchy of values, or whether they should act only from the point of view of their own subjective interests.

The other extreme answer is that criteria for distributive justice can be adopted at will, since all justice means is that these criteria should be seen as generally valid, and not dictated by subjective interests. There is a way in which this answer is valid. If the Tibetans elect a certain child to be Dalai Lama because it has a particular birthmark, there is no sense in regarding this process as being unjust in itself. So

42

long as it is based upon a generally held conviction that a divine power has used this sign to make it known to the world who should be the bearer of spiritual and temporal power, then the most one can criticize is the truth of the belief, not the justness of the criteria of selection. It would only be unjust if the priest carrying out the examination proclaimed the son of a particular family to be Dalai Lama, although the child did not have the birthmark. So it is true that justice is found first and foremost in impartiality.

Yet it is possible, in enlightened civilizations, and with regard to most aspects of all civilizations, to distinguish between relevant and irrelevant criteria for distribution. When deciding who should study medicine it is obvious that neither parental wealth, nor a father who is a party-functionary, nor political activity in a youth organization, nor even 'A' level grades are the relevant criteria. That is why some people nowadays are thinking in terms of aptitude tests. It would be relevant for example to see how a candidate got on in a trial period as an orderly in a hospital, as well as making sure he or she had the necessary intelligence. Even the fact that someone's father or mother was a doctor could count, not unjustly, as a relevant secondary criterion. At least this would not be as unjust as the distinction of having won a lottery. Different relevant points of view often conflict and it is difficult to establish any form of hierarchy. One could take as an example the present discussions in West Germany about child benefit or tax-free allowances for children. Those in favour of the lump benefit say that although the rich get more out of it than the poor, or rather the less well-off, nonetheless, all children are worth just as much as each other and, besides, poorer people need the money for their children more urgently than the rich. The other party argues that since well-off people not only pay more tax than the less well-off in absolute terms, but also in percentage terms, the benefit should be seen not as a free gift, but just as a way of lightening of the burden. Finally they argue that it is in fact inevitable that rich people will spend more on their children, because the children will participate in the general standard of living of the family. Without the benefit the wealthy would be forced to lower their standard of living disproportionately, in a way which would in fact punish the children. I do not want to go into this discussion any further, but to use it as an example of how different criteria of distributive justice can compete with one another.

The philosophers of antiquity were well aware of this sort of conflict. They spoke of proportional and arithmetical equality. Arithmetical equality means that everyone gets the same. This does not mean getting the same reward for the same peformance, but that all get the same reward regardless of achievement. Therefore everyone would have the same chance of getting high-ranking government posts regardless of qualifications. It is obvious that this would be unjust. No one would want to live in a state where doctors get their qualifications not as a result of painstaking medical studies but win them in lotteries in which everyone can take part.

The converse principle is that of proportional equality. Marx expressed this in the formula, 'From each according to his abilities, to each according to his achievements'. This principle of 'to each his own', rather than 'to each the same', is in some ways closer to justice than the arithmetical view, but it is still not satisfactory as it stands. This is firstly because it does not answer the question of how we should evaluate performance, whether this should be according to the amount of trouble taken, inconvenience, the amount of qualifications required, or whatever. Then the fact remains that getting qualifications to carry out certain highly-regarded jobs is itself partially the result of chance opportunities, beginning with the fact that some people happen to be talented, and continuing with the fact that one person may have been stopped, as a result of physical or psychological handicap, from achieving certain things, whilst another person was not. That is why Plato wrote that only God could operate exclusively in terms of proportional justice, because He alone would be able to judge the absolute value of each individual and his achievements. Human beings on the other hand should constantly moderate different competing standards by recourse to arithmetical equality, for otherwise justice could very easily turn into injustice. A pure meritocracy would be every bit as unjust as a society which disregards achievement and leaves it unrewarded.

Besides arithmetical equality and proportionality based on achievement there is another form of proportionality which is appropriate in a just society, and that is the proportionality which is related to human need. This principle came into the world through Christianity. It says that whoever is not able to help themselves should be helped in proportion to their needs. It says that it is not unjust to ask the majority to provide the means for this, and this does not mean in an ideal consumer society in an imaginary future, but in the here and now. This proportionality has to do with what we call loving one's neighbour, and to a certain extent this idea of neighbourly love definitely has passed into our ideas about justice. There is no doubt that what the Good Samaritan did when he paid personally to have the severely injured victims cared for at the inn goes beyond the requirements of mere justice. Still, the priests and Levites who saw the injured man and walked past could, under our penal code, be brought to trial and charged with neglecting to offer assistance. That is a step forward.

Chapter five

Conviction and responsibility: does the end justify the means?

We began to consider what it is to act in a just way towards others. We have not yet found an answer to this question but we have pointed out an important pre-requisite of justice. This is the sort of attitude of mind which makes a person distributing or laying claim to scarce goods ready and able to be detached about personal preferences and sympathies and to apply criteria which can be justified to all other parties involved. If this is so, we can go on to say that inequalities of distribution must be justified. They must be proportioned according to relevant qualities and should not arise out of discrimination between persons or groups of persons which those involved would never be able to agree to. Justice means recognizing that every person is worthy of respect for his or her own sake.

'Justice' in itself though is not enough if we are to 'do justice' to our fellow human beings. If a government were to forbid everyone, including its own members, to smell roses, it would not be acting unjustly, because it would not be discriminating against people on irrelevant grounds; but such a prohibition would nonetheless be quite idiotic. The story of Solomon's judgment gives us an impressive example of the fact that there is something higher than justice. Two women bring before the king their quarrel about which of them should have care of the sole survivor of their children. Solomon is not in a position to clear up the matter directly, so he orders the baby to be cut in two with a sword and for one piece to be given to each of the women. The woman who cries out against this and is ready to let the other woman keep the child is the one Solomon recognizes as the true mother. She gives up her claim to justice because she loves the child. The ancient story disregards the fact that the child also has a claim to justice. It deals only with the question of justice between the two women. It is nonetheless a generally valid principle that it is immoral to want to destroy goods which cannot be distributed justly rather than finding some grounds for giving them to someone. Even if no relevant grounds can be found, there is always the possibility of drawing lots or taking into consideration the rights of the person in whose possession they happen to be at the time.

Dealing justly with people and with reality goes beyond mere justice. Two further things are required, knowledge and love. Without knowledge about what man is and what is good for him we cannot act correctly. A person who spoils a child with too many sweets or too much television may well love that child, but he is doing just what someone would do who wished to harm the child. Knowledge informed by love is best. If one person wishes to harm another, knowledge is bad, because the more someone knows, the more damage he is able to do. The sort of love we are talking about here is not the same as sympathy. Whether or not we feel sympathy is not something over which we have power. Love is more like goodwill, willing that others should come to have whatever is good for them. Such goodwill is not directed only towards human beings but towards all living things. To inflict needless pain on an animal is to be unjust to it. It is in the nature of pain that no one should want to inflict it, because no one would want to suffer it.

The next thing we need to know is what this general readiness to do justice to reality, and particularly to other people, actually requires of us. We need to know what demands are made by this goodwill, without which there can be no good life. We need to know what standards we should apply to our actions, over and above justice, for us to be able to call them good. There has been a long philosophical controversy over this, to which we must now turn. The great sociologist Max Weber characterized two possible approaches, which he thought were irreconcilable, using the terms 'ethics of conviction' and 'ethics of responsibility'.

By ethics of responsibility he meant the attitude of a person who determines how he should act by taking into account the totality of foreseeable consequences, that is, by considering which set of consequences taken together in the context of the value content of reality are best. That person will act accordingly even if it means doing something which, taken in isolation, would appear to be a bad action. A doctor would be acting in accordance with what Weber termed ethics of responsibility if he lied to a patient about the state of his or her health, for fear that the patient would not be able to bear the truth. So too a politician would be acting according to ethics of responsibility if he builds up the country's capacity for war, and indeed prepares for the eventuality of having to wage war, in order that this should have a deterrent effect, thereby decreasing the actual likelihood of war.

The pacifist on the other hand subscribes to ethics of conviction, so long as he says that he is not prepared to kill under any circumstances, not even if the spread of pacifism on one side were to increase the danger of war. His argument is that if all people were pacifists there would be no war at all, and that someone has got to start somewhere. If it were put to him that pacifism was unlikely to become general, but have the effect only of weakening one side to the extent that a potential enemy might seize the opportunity of starting a war, the pacifist's reply would be that this would not be his fault, and if people were going to start killing each other, then he would not want any part in it.

Max Weber was of the opinion that these two points of view were at absolutely opposite poles and were irreconcilable by means of rational argument. He was inclined to see the ethics of responsibility as being appropriate to the politician and the ethics of conviction as appropriate to the saint. This of course does not take into account the fact that there have been politicians who were at once saintly and successful, though these, admittedly, have been few and far between.

In modern ethics this problem is often discussed in terms of the contrast between deontological and teleological systems of ethics. 'Deontological' is the name given to systems of ethics which regard certain actions as good or bad in general, regardless of their consequences. 'Teleological' systems calculate the moral worth of actions in terms of the value of the totality of their probable consequences. 'Utilitarianism' is another name given to teleological moral systems, or ethics of responsibility.

Talking in terms of a contrast between ethics of conviction and ethics of responsibility, or between deontology and utilitarianism, in fact tends to obscure the issues under discussion. One is reminded of something Hegel said: 'The principle that we should act in a way which disregards consequences, and the contrary principle that we should judge actions according to consequences and make these judgments the measure of what is just and good, both arise out of an abstract form of understanding'.

There is in fact no system of ethics which absolutely disregards the consequences of actions, because it is not possible to define an action without making reference to particular effects. Action means 'bringing about effects'. If for example you regard all lies as being in principle reprehensible, this does not mean that you are disregarding consequences. What you are really doing is taking into account one consequence only, the very consequence that makes a lie a lie, the deception or misleading of another person. Without this consequence there would be no lies, otherwise telling fairy-tales would be telling lies. So it is not a question of conviction or responsibility, nor is it a question of taking into account or disregarding consequences. The question is which consequences of his actions an agent should bear responsibility for and how far into the future it is legitimate to see these consequences extending. The question is whether there are specific consequences which should never be permitted, or whether, on the contrary, any action is permissible if, in the long term, the totality of the positive consequences justifies it. So, finally, it comes down to the old question of whether or not the end justifies the means, if a particular good end seems to outweigh the harm caused by the means.

Now there is no doubt that most of what we do depends on the way we weigh up the consequences, or the goods which are positively or negatively affected by the consequences of our actions. We weigh up pros and cons. There are occasions when a doctor will amputate a leg or remove a kidney in order to save the rest of the patient, or he might forbid a patient the pleasure of drinking wine, in order to save the patient from consequences even more unpleasant than not drinking. Here there is no doubt that the end justifies the means; these are examples of ethics of responsibility.

What happens though if we pursue this way of thinking unchecked? If for example a doctor is treating an ill-natured person, who gets on his own nerves and on the nerves of everyone about him, or if, say, he is treating a criminal, should the doctor, being responsible for the sum total of the consequences, prescribe a course of treatment which will finish the patient off as soon as possible? In this way Soviet psychiatrists can be said to be practising ethics of responsibility when they lock away dissidents in asylums and treat them with drugs designed to break their will, since they are considered to be dangerous people. This sort of behaviour radically contradicts our understanding of a doctor's responsibility, which is that it should extend no further than the final goal of doing what is best for the patient's health. Any subordination of this concern to more extensive responsibilities for other consequences would not be reconcilable with medical ethics.

It would also be irreconcilable with medical ethics if, for example, a doctor testing drugs, who knew before the end of an experiment that these drugs would save the lives of some patients, withheld these drugs from a control group. The relationship between doctor and patient depends on a tacit agreement that no ulterior goals and no more far-reaching consequences than the patient's recovery will play a rôle during the course of the patient's treatment. But a different situation arises when scarcity of resources intervenes. If for example there are not enough heart–lung machines or artificial kidneys available for all who need them, then a decision has to be made according to the criteria of distributive justice. That is to say that there are circumstances under which one actually does have to weigh up one life against another from an objective and impartial point of view.

Such examples are often introduced in order to prove that the weighing up of goods or values is a general characteristic of our moral behaviour. Yet it would be wrong to draw such a conclusion. The form of utilitarianism which holds this to be the case is untenable for several reasons, as the following reflections should briefly show.

Utilitarianism fails first of all because of the complexity and unpredictability of the long-term consequences of our actions. If we did have to take into account all the consequences of our actions, we would spend so much time trying to work these out that we would never get round to doing anything at all. The lowering of infant mortality rates in poorer countries often has catastrophic consequences in the long term, but then these in turn lead to further pressure to improve overall living conditions, though it is not clear whether or not this is possible. Who can judge what, finally, will turn out to have been the most important consideration? No one would do anything at all if they had, beforehand, to take all that into account.

Conversely it is often the case that in the long term good can come out of bad. Jesus said specifically that Judas' betrayal of him was not justified by the fact that it turned out to be a means to the redemption of mankind. Every crime would be justified if the person committing it was pursuing an end which 'justified' the means. We are dealing here with a very peculiar dialectic. What Max Weber called the radical ethics of responsibility is in reality nothing less than the radical ethics of conviction. For according to this way of thinking we can no longer judge an action in itself, but we should take into account the outlook and the intentions of the agent and the way he sees the final goal of history; then it would be possible, because of his convictions, to absolve him from blame for actions, which would normally be regarded as crimes. As such, subscribing to ethics of responsibility can be seen as tantamount to believing in a radical form of ethics of conviction. The truth of the matter is that when it comes to trying to work out what all the consequences will be, we are always groping in the dark. If the morality of our actions did depend on making judgments of that nature, then we would have to cry out, with Hamlet, 'The time is out of joint; O cursed spite, That ever I was born to set it right!'

The second argument is that utilitarianism sacrifices the moral judgments of ordinary individuals to the technical intelligence of experts, and that it changes moral norms into technical norms. Utilitarianism makes it impossible to see the moral qualities of actions in the actions themselves because of the need to refer to a universal utility function. Experts are needed in order to determine this, even though these experts may be self-appointed. When young SS men during the Nazi regime were ordered to kill Jewish children, this might have troubled the conscience of some of them. Their conscience though was silenced by theories like the one that, in the long run, the existence of Jews was harmful to mankind. Even if we assume that some of them may have been too stupid or too deluded to see through the absurdity of this theory, they should still have borne with the simple insight that one should not kill innocent children.

But utilitarianism does not allow for the validity of such simple insights. Conscience is placed under the tutelage of ideologists and technocrats. In case anyone thinks that the above example is too extreme to have any meaning for us, it is worth calling to mind the Milgram experiment, first carried out by Professor Milgram in the United States in the early 1970s and later repeated by Bavarian Radio. A number of people were chosen at random from the street, young and old, men and women, and they were asked to take part in an experiment which they were told would be of great significance in developing methods of learning. In the course of this experiment the people in question had to administer electric shocks to a human guinea-pig in an enclosed room by pressing a button, gradually increasing the strength of the shock. I should add of course that the whole experiment was simulated. No one really got an electric shock. Only the passers-by taking part in the experiment thought that they did. The passers-by were the real subjects of the experiment. The idea was to see how far they were prepared to go in taking part in the experiment. The frightening thing was that they were prepared to go a very long way. When the supposed human guinea-pig began to scream and the supposed electric shock approached lethal dosage there were some who wanted to stop. It was then explained to them that if they did not continue, the whole expensive project would be ruined, but on the other hand if the experiment were to succeed it would bring about a significant improvement in methods of learning throughout the world. Most of them allowed their conscience to be disarmed by this utilitarian argument and carried on with their job as torturers.

This experiment leads us to the conclusion that trying to determine our actions by consideration of the sum total of the consequences disorientates people and makes them open to all sorts of temptations and possibilities of manipulation. Because this will obviously not lead to a better world, the utilitarian ends up contradicting himself; what he wants is the best of all possible worlds. The problem is that the best possible world is not likely to be achieved if all people make it their aim to bring it about.

Even from a utilitarian point of view, trying to act in accordance with utilitarian criteria is likely to do more harm that good.

A third argument should make this even more clear. The utilitarian is not only easily led astray by so-called experts; it is also easier for criminals to blackmail him. This in turn increases the likelihood of blackmail. Of course in some cases it is right, according to utilitarian criteria, to stand up to blackmail, in order to bring blackmail itself into abeyance. And yet it is necessary, on each separate occasion, to weigh up the balance of possible evils, in order to see whether or not one should give in. The private individual would be more ready to give in, and rightly so, than the politician who is duty-bound to take into account more long term consequences. A politician's actions, more than those of anyone else, have to follow utilitarian criteria derived from the 'ethics of responsibility'. The moral problem becomes most vividly clear in cases where a blackmailer demands *criminal* action, for example the killing of an innocent person or the handing over of someone to whom one has duties as a guest, in order to avoid the threat of far greater evil. Under such circumstances the utilitarian would have to give in on the grounds that the death of one person would be better than the death of a hundred persons. But if you consider it a crime to kill any one innocent person under any circumstances you will not be so impressed by this logic. Moreover, if it is known that this is your point of view, then it will be less likely that anyone will try to blackmail you in the first place. So here again we come across circumstances where utilitarianism can be counter-productive, that is to say, where it can bring about the very consequences it seeks to avoid.

The result of the arguments so far seems to be that our moral responsibility can only be realistic, definite and beyond arbitrary manipulation, if it is at the same time limited, that is, if we do not start from the position that we have always to be responsible for the sum total of the consequences of all our acts and omissions. It is only in terms of this presupposition that we can define the word 'omission'. Criminal negligence is the omission of something which ought to have been done. If we were responsible every moment for everything that we were not doing at that moment, and if we had to examine every single alternative course of action and choose the best one every single time we acted at all, the demands on us would be impossible.

Establishing the exact extent of an agent's responsibility in every case would be a very long and complicated process. For example the responsibility of a doctor is of a more limited nature than that of a politician, who must be expected and permitted to consider very far-reaching and complex sequences of consequences. Yet even the politician's duty to seek out the best is related primarily to the territory for which he or she has real responsibility. Politicians do not have to care for other countries in the sense that they have to do the best for them; their duty towards them is rather that they should deal justly with them.

The question remains as to whether there is such a thing as a responsibility which every human being has simply through being human, a responsibility which all human beings have. There is also the question as to whether there are certain actions which deny this responsibility. Kant formulated this universal demand by saying that we should never act in such a way as to use ourselves or others merely as means. It is possible to object that in fact we always need each other as means to certain ends, that the whole common life of humanity depends on this. But of course Kant was well aware of this. What he meant was that we should only ever use each other partially as means. We may indeed profit from the capacities and achievements of others, but at the same time we should remain aware of the fact that the other person is also an end-in-himself and also has the right to claim certain services from his fellow human beings. So his rights as a person are not denied. Yet there are certain ways of behaving which do deny a human being's rights as a person. For example a person is not being treated as an end-in-himself if he is sold into slavery, or if he is tortured, or killed for no reason, or is sexually abused, and also, as Kant thought, if he is deliberately deceived, though there are problems with this latter point which I do not want to discuss here.

The point is that the relationship between good and bad actions is asymmetrical. This is because there is no action which could, at all times and in all places, count as 'good'. How good an action is always depends on the sum total of circumstances. This explains how it is that we can regard the omission of a bad action as being something 'good'. However there are certain actions which are, regardless of the circumstances, bad, at all times and in all places, because by their very nature they deny the quality of a person as an end-in-him- or -herself, that is to say, they deny a person's dignity. With such actions there is no more room for calculating consequences. This means that we cannot be held responsible for the omission of actions which are in themselves bad. If a soldier refused to shoot a Jewish girl who was begging him for her life, and his commanding officer threatened to shoot ten people if he still refused, it is not the soldier who would be responsible for the deaths of those people, but the commanding officer. After all, we all have to die one day, but we do not have to commit murder.

We are no more responsible for not doing what we should not do than we are for not doing what we are physically unable to do. Someone whose conscience transformed 'I may not' into 'I cannot', would be a good person. The Ancient Roman legislator formulated this clearly when he wrote, 'Whatever offends against piety, or against respect for human beings, in short against good morals, should be regarded as impossible.'

Chapter six

The individual: should we always follow our conscience?

Until now we have been discussing the different perspectives which come into play when we call an action good or bad, right or wrong, successful or unsuccessful. We have considered the question of what we truly and fundamentally want and we have tried to see the good in terms of the satisfaction of our true desires. We have talked of values, of the consequences of actions and of justice. However it does seem that there might be one simple, clear answer which would make all such considerations superfluous. This is that we are told what we should do by our conscience.

This is a correct answer but at the same time it is misleading in its simplicity. The next task is to consider it more closely by asking questions like what 'conscience' actually is, what it does, whether it is always right, whether it should always be obeyed and whether or not we should always respect the conscience of others.

The word 'conscience' obviously does not have just one simple meaning. It is used in very different contexts. We use the word 'conscientious' to describe people who are punctilious in their daily duties; but we also use the word 'conscience' to explain why certain people break out of their daily round of duties to fight for what they believe in. We talk of conscience as something sacred which all human beings possess and which we have an absolute duty to respect. It is protected by the West German constitution, and yet severe criminal punishments are still meted out to those who commit so-called 'crimes of conscience'. Some think conscience is the voice of God in man. Others think it is the product of upbringing, the internalization of learnt norms derived from originally external power structures. What does all this add up to?

The concept of conscience implies the idea of human dignity. It means seeing the human person not as a specific case of a generality or as a specimen of a species, but regarding each individual as a self-contained totality, as the generality itself.

It makes sense to regard the natural law which says that stones fall as something which lies outside the stone itself. The stone knows nothing about it. It is we, the observers, who see the falling of the stone as an example of the general rule. Birds do not build nests because they have in mind the intention to perpetuate the species or because they are planning for the care of their future offspring. They are driven by an inner urge, an instinct, to do something, the meaning of which is hidden from them. This can be seen from the fact that birds in captivity, who have no possibility of having children, set about building nests.

People on the other hand are capable of knowing why it is they do what they do. Our relationship to our actions is free and explicit. If we desire to do something, the consequences of which will be harmful to others, we can reflect upon these consequences and ask ourselves if it is right to act in this way and whether or not we are prepared to accept responsibility. We are capable of detaching ourselves from the subjective interests of the moment and calling to mind the objective hierarchy of values relevant to our actions. We do not do this on a purely theoretical level, in such a way that insights we gain from our deliberations remain external to us and have no effect on our actions. For example we do not say, 'It may well be unjust to act in such a way from an objective point of view, but it is still in my interests to do so'. In reality what we basically, really, want is not fundamentally opposed to what is good and right. When conscience comes into play, what we spontaneously want actually is this general viewpoint, the objective hierarchy of different types of good and the challenge of taking all this into account. Conscience is a demand we make upon ourselves. If we harm, wrong, or injure another person, we also directly harm ourselves. We are left with what we call a 'bad conscience'.

The conscience is the focal point of an absolute perspective in a finite being, the means by which this perspective is anchored in that being's emotional structure. It is because of this presence of the universal, the objective, the absolute, in the individual person, that we talk of human dignity; there is no other reason. So if it is through his conscience that man, individual man, attains to a universal status and becomes what one might call a meaningful whole, then it must follow that it is impossible for man to perceive anything as good, or as having any sense or justification, unless what actually is right and good can be revealed to him as being such by his conscience.

Conscience has to be described as a twofold movement of the spirit. On the one hand it leads man beyond himself; it allows him to perceive his own interests as something relative and to ask himself what is good and right. Also, to be sure of freedom from self-deception, his relationship with others must involve constant exchange of information and ideas about goodness and justice, that is to say, he has to live in the moral community. He has to take arguments and counter-arguments into account. If anyone says they are not interested in moral standards because they know already what is right and good, this shows that they are neither objective nor universal in their way of thinking. It is not possible to distinguish what such a person refers to as his conscience from private moods and other sorts of idiosyncratic behaviour.

There is no such thing as a conscience which is not prepared to submit itself to further education or to take on board further information. A doctor who did not keep up with developments in medical science would not be acting in good conscience, nor would people who deliberately blocked out of their minds the views of others trying to point out aspects of their actions they had not perhaps been aware of. If it were not part of the nature of conscience to re-examine itself it would only make sense to talk about conscience in the context of some borderline cases.

Conscience is characterized also by a second type of movement which leads the individual back again to himself. If, as I said, the individual is potentially a universal, meaningful whole, he cannot offload responsibility for his actions onto other people, or the customs of the day, or the anonymity of rational discourse, or the weighing up of pros and cons. Of course he can adopt whatever the prevailing opinion happens to be, and indeed, in most cases that is the most reasonable thing to do. It is quite wrong to attribute conscience only to those who do not follow the majority. Yet in the final analysis it is always the individual himself who bears the responsibility. He can obey authority, and it may well be right and reasonable to do so; but it is the *person* in question who, in the last analysis, has to account for his decision to obey. Discussions of pros and cons are always possible. The trouble is though that such discussions can go on forever. Human life on the other hand is finite. We need to be able to act despite the fact that there may as yet be no world-wide agreement about right and wrong. So the individual has to decide when the time is right to step out of the endless process of weighing up arguments, bring the discussion to an end and act, finally, with conviction.

This conviction, which makes it possible to put a stop to deliberation, is what we call conscience. It does not always consist in the certainty that we are doing what is objectively for the best. Politicians, doctors, fathers and mothers do not always know with absolute certainty whether or not they are giving the best possible advice in terms of possible consequences. But they are in a position to know that they are giving the best possible advice in terms of what they know at the time. This is enough to satisfy conscience, because, as we have already seen, an action is not justified, nor could it possibly be justified, in terms of the sum total of its consequences.

With conscience we seem to detach ourselves entirely from outside influence. But is that really what we do? A complicated problem crops up here. The question is how this guiding compass called conscience came to be inside us and how, or by whom, it was programmed. Perhaps this internal guide is in fact nothing more than remote control exercised by an external source, namely the past. The guidance-equipment we possess may well have been programmed by, say, our parents. In this case it could be said that the norms we were introduced to in childhood and which we had to obey, were internalized by us in such a way that commands given to us by others became commands we give to ourselves.

It was in this connection that Freud coined the term 'super-ego', which he saw as forming the structure of our personality, along with the so-called 'id' and 'ego'. The super-ego is, so to speak, the internalized father image, the father within. For Freud this did not have the same pejorative character which neo-marxist social criticism later ascribed to the internalization of dominant social norms. As a psychoanalyst, Freud observed that it was only under the influence of the super-ego that the ego was able to take shape and free itself from the constraints of instinctive drives, that is, from the id. But it was also absolutely necessary for it to free itself from domination by the super-ego in order to become a true self or ego.

However pertinent we may see Freud's descriptions as being, it would still be mistaken simply to identify what we call conscience with the super-ego or to regard conscience as being no more than a product of upbringing. This is because there always have been and always will be people who react against the norms which are dominant in their society, the norms they grew up with. This happens even if their fathers in some way embodied these norms. It could be said that what lies behind this reaction is nothing more than the ego's desire for emancipation, a simple reflex-desire to be different, and it would be true that this sort of reflex-desire would have no more to do with conscience than a reflex-desire to conform.

Yet throughout the course of history we observe that people who really did act or refuse to act on grounds of conscience were not by nature given to contrariness or to dissent. They would rather have carried on with their daily lives without fuss. 'A true servant of my King, but God's servant first' was the by-word of Sir Thomas More. He did everything he could to co-operate with the king and avoid conflict, right up to the point where he was asked to sign something he was absolutely unable to square with his conscience. He was guided neither by a need to conform, nor by a need to dissent, but by the calm conviction that there are some things one simply should not do. He identified this conviction so much with his own self that for him 'should not' became 'cannot'.

If conscience is not a product of upbringing, and if it is not identical with the super-ego, then maybe it is innate, a kind of in-born instinct of a social nature. Yet this cannot be right either because instincts are obeyed 'instinctively'. A person driven by instinct who says he can 'do no other' is as different as night is from day to a person acting out of conscience saying the same thing. The person who is driven by instinct feels literally driven, unfree; he would like to be able to want to do something else, but cannot. He is discontented with himself. But when the person acting in accordance with his conscience says 'Here I stand and can do no other', he is giving expression to his freedom. He is saying something like, 'I don't want anything else. I cannot want anything else and I do not want to be able to want anything else.' A man like that is free. He is, as the Greeks used to say, friends with himself.

Where does conscience come from then? We may as well ask where language comes from or why we speak. It is obvious that we speak because we learnt how to do so from our parents. Anyone who hears no speech remains dumb,

62

and anyone who never takes part in any form of communication cannot even be said to be able to think, because our thoughts are a kind of inner speech. And yet no one would say that language is a form of external determination which has become internalized.

What is 'self-determination'? It would be wrong to say that a human person, taken in isolation, is not a thinking, speaking being. The truth of the matter is that a human person is a being who needs the help of others in order to become what he really is. The same is true of conscience. In every human being there is a predisposition to develop a conscience, a kind of faculty by means of which good and bad are known. This can be seen clearly in the way children behave, as anyone who has had anything to do with them will know. They have a developed sense of justice. They become outraged if they see justice violated. They have a sense of whether a musical note is in tune or not, and they have a sense of what is good and proper. But unless these values are embodied in some form of authority, this faculty withers away. If they are placed too soon in a situation where all that counts is the right of the strongest, they lose their sense of fairness, their delicacy of feeling and their openness. Initially, the word, language, is a means by which truth becomes explicit. But if children are cowed by threats and if they learn that they have to lie in order escape punishment, or if they learn that their parents tell them untruths and that in everyday life lying is a normal means of getting what you want, then the lustre vanishes, and only stunted forms of conscience develop. Conscience becomes coarsened. A delicate, sensitive conscience is the sign of an inwardly open and free person. This has nothing to do with the ways of the moral pedant who, instead of looking to the right and the good, looks only to himself and suspiciously scrutinizes his every step. That is a form of sickness.

There are those who think all bad conscience is a form of sickness. They see it as the psychologist's job to free us from bad conscience, from so-called guilt feelings. Yet in reality it is a form of sickness not to be capable of having a bad conscience or guilt feelings if one actually is guilty of something, in the same way that it is an illness, a mortally dangerous illness, to be unable to feel pain. Pain is a sign of danger to life and as such it serves to protect life. It would be true to call someone sick who felt pain without organic causes. In the same way the moral pedant who suffers from a guilty conscience without actually being guilty is also sick. In a healthy person a guilty conscience is a sign of guilt, that is to say of an attitude of mind which stands in contradiction both to the nature of his own being and to the nature of reality.

'Repentance' is the name given to the process of putting this relationship back into order. As the philosopher Max Scheler showed, repentance does not just mean senselessly rummaging in the past when it would make more sense simply to do better in future. It is in fact impossible to do better in future if you have the same attitude of mind that caused you to act wrongly in the first place. The past should not be repressed. It has to be faced up to. This means making a conscious effort to alter wrong attitudes. Since human attitudes are not just a matter of the head, but of emotions also, changing attitudes imply experiencing pain at harm one has done. The psychologist Mitscherlich talks of the working out of sorrow. In fact repentance is something we come to expect. If someone torments a child, making of it a spiritual cripple, and then laughingly declares that once is enough and that he will treat the next child well, we would not trust him. If he feels no pain about the past, if he is not gripped and changed by a guilty conscience, that means he is still the same person he was.

Is conscience always right? That was the first question we asked. Then we asked if we should always follow our conscience. Our conscience is not always right. We cannot rely on our conscience any more than we can rely on our five senses always to lead us in the right direction, or on our reason always to preserve us from error. Conscience is a human faculty for recognizing good and evil; it is not an oracle. It shows us the way, it causes us to look beyond our egoistic perspectives towards the universal and towards that which is right in itself. But reaching this viewpoint requires reflection, expertise and, if I may say so, moral expertise. This involves a correct sense of the structure of the hierarchy of values, which is not distorted by ideologies.

Consciences are sometimes in error. There are those who act out of conscience who sometimes do seriously wrong others. Should they follow their conscience? Of course. Man's dignity lies, as we saw, in his being a meaningful whole. The good and the right have to be perceived by man as good before they can actually be good. As such it is not right to say that for man there could be something which is *only objectively* good. If a person does not perceive something as good, then for that person it is not good. He has to follow his conscience. All this means is that he has to do what he *considers* to be objectively good, which is of course quite obvious. That is why it would be true to say that what is really good is only that which is right both objectively and subjectively.

We might try to establish criteria by means of which we could decide whether or not a conscience was in error. But how could this be possible? If it were, none would ever be in error. Indeed a good indication that someone is following their conscience and not just some whim is their readiness to check their own judgment with others, their readiness to change their minds or indeed to stand up for what they believe. But not even that is a foolproof test. One might take the opposite example of a person surrounded by people intellectually superior or more articulate than himself, who still has the certain feeling that these people were in the wrong, without, however, being able to fathom exactly why. The person in question would not actually think the others had better reasons for their beliefs, only that he was not the right person to argue through the reasons for his convictions. He would see it merely as an unhappy accident of the particular situation that the more intelligent people were on the wrong side. In situations like that putting up a barrier to defend oneself against the reasoning of others can be an act of conscience.

The next question is whether the consciences of others should always be respected. The answer depends on what is meant by 'respected'. Under no circumstances can this mean that everyone must be allowed to do what their conscience permits them. In that case the person with no conscience would be allowed to do anything. It cannot mean either that everyone should be allowed to do what their conscience tells them to do. Certainly everyone has a duty follow their conscience. But if in doing so a person infringes the rights of others, then both the others and the state have the right to stand in his way. It is an important element in human rights that the rights of one person should not be made dependent on the way the conscience of another person judges a situation. There is no reason why one should not discuss the question of the legal rights of unborn children, even if the West German constitution already gives a positive answer to it. However, slogans stating that this should be decided by the conscience of individuals are nonsensical. Either it is the case that unborn children have no right to life, in which case there is no need even to mention conscience, or else the unborn do have a right to life, in which case the right cannot be made to depend on the disposition of other peoples' consciences.

Nor is it possible to limit obedience of the laws of a constitutional state, which the majority of its citizens regard as just, to those whose conscience does not prohibit, for example, the payment of taxes. People who fail to pay taxes but still use the roads and sewage systems at the expense of others, are fined or punished. If they really are acting out of conscience, they will accept the punishment.

It is only with regard to military service that legislators in West Germany made a ruling guaranteeing that no one should be forced to serve against his conscience. This legislation is basically trivial, for if someone's conscience forbids him to fight, he will not fight. Even here there are no criteria by means of which it can be decided from the outside whether or not someone is acting out of conscience. Judicial hearings are not an appropriate way of facilitating judgments in this sort of case. In the final analysis they are bound only to favour cleverer speakers who are prepared to lie and are adept at lying.

There is only one indication of the genuineness of a decision to act out of conscience and that is the readiness of the person concerned to face unpleasant alternatives. A person's conscience is not infringed if he is stopped from doing something which his conscience tells him to. He bears no responsibility for the fact that he was stopped from doing it. That is why it is both permissible and right to lock away a person who wants to make the world a better place by criminal means. But the situation is different in the case of someone being actively forced to act against his conscience. This offends human dignity, given, of course, that it is possible. Not even the threat of death can actually force a person to act against his conscience, as stories of martyrs throughout the ages bear witness.

Yet there is one way in which people can be forced to act against their conscience, and this is the sort of torture which makes a person an involuntary tool of others. That is why torture is counted amongst the small number of actions which are always and under all circumstances bad. This is because it directly violates the sanctuary of the conscience, about which the pre-Christian philosopher Seneca wrote, 'There dwells within us a sacred spirit which watches over and observes our deeds, both good and bad'.

Chapter seven

The unconditional: what makes an action good?

We have seen that nothing which goes against conscience can be good. We also saw that it does not follow from this that everything which happens in accordance with conscience is good, because conscience is not an oracle but a faculty. As such it can be led astray. Moreover, no form of introspection and no amount of delving in our own inner depths can tell us if the voice we hear really is conscience. No one judging from the outside can determine whether or not someone really is acting out of conscience, and even we ourselves cannot be absolutely sure of this. Man looks towards the good by means of conscience, but he cannot see the eye with which he looks. We have to follow what we believe we see.

Kant wrote: 'It is impossible to conceive anything at all in the world, or even out of it, which can be taken as good without qualification, except a *good will*.' If we keep to the terms of this sentence, then we immediately have to ask what a good will is. Obviously it is a will which wills the good. But this shows that the question about what the good is cannot be answered simply by means of reference to the good will. The conventional wisdom that good intent is in the end the most important thing is by no means as harmless as it at first appears. It can easily be used to justify every kind of injustice and wickedness.

There is a certain sense in which everyone acts with good intent. No one wants what is bad because it is bad. Everyone wants something positive, some sort of value, be this pleasure, spiritual satisfaction, perhaps even the happiness of another person, more justice, or whatever. Plato and philosophers after him throughout antiquity and the Middle Ages held that action was only possible if it was in pursuit of something good, some value. They held that evil, or the bad, came about if someone who was pursuing a particular good unjustifiably caused harm, or allowed for harm to be caused. This was seen especially to be the case if the wrongdoer left it to someone else to pay the cost, for example someone stealing in order later to be able to make munificent gifts to charity. A good intention does not stop an action from being unjust.

Besides, justifying actions only in terms of so-called good intentions is bound to lead to deceit. As I have said, we never want evil for evil's sake, but only ever as a means or as something we might allow to happen in the pursuit of some other aim which is not in itself bad. If all actions were justified only by good intentions, then the most innocent person would be the one who successfully avoided thinking consciously about the negative aspects of his actions. We are all aware of doing just this. If we attempt to do something we should not do, something we ought really not even want to do, then, in general, we try to divert our attention from the negative aspects of the action and direct it only to the positive aspects.

Conscience makes it more difficult for us to put such considerations out of our minds, by reminding us of all the aspects of our actions. Conscience calls upon us to be more aware. A will can only be called good if it allows conscience to compel it to face up to the whole reality of the action in question, without using some kind of so-called good intention as a means of deceiving itself. It would be possible to define evil as a refusal to pay attention. There is a sense in which someone who acts badly does not know what he is doing. The point, though, is that he does not want to know. It is here, rather than in intentions which are obviously bad, that evil is to be found.

Perhaps now we could make an attempt at giving an indirect answer to the question of what makes an action good. This would be that whether or not an action is good must have something to do with the quality of attention and the clarity of vision with which we look upon reality. There are many things which can cloud our vision, enthralment by some captivating desire of the moment, sensuality, striving for power, even ideals. What else does an inquisitor get out of the death of a heretic? What does the terrorist get out of his way of life and the fear it inspires? The only answer can be that these things satisfy some sort of idealism. These people refuse to direct their attention to what their actions mean to those on the receiving end of them. This does not apply only to inquisitors and terrorists, but to every one of us when we get so carried away by a desire to do something useful, helpful, or loving that we divert our attention from the fact that we are leaving it to someone else to pay the cost for our noble impulses. This someone, because, for example, of a promise of loyalty we might have made to them, could well be the very person to whom we really owe what are giving to others.

Yet perhaps we should see the good itself as a kind of ideal. If so, what does it consist in? Asking careless questions like 'what does the good consist in?' causes difficulties. Plato used to say that good actions were good because of their goodness; and that is obviously a tautology. Yet in some respects it is an unavoidable tautology. G. E. Moore made a thorough investigation of attempts to re-express what we mean when we call something good using different terms. To make such an attempt was to commit what he called the 'naturalistic fallacy'. The results are as misleading as attempts to reduce what we mean by terms like 'blue', 'quiet', or 'pain' to other concepts. Neither health, nor the good of the fatherland, nor improving one's standard of living, nor egoism, nor altruism sum up absolutely what we mean by the good. This can be shown in terms of the logical considerations dealt with in the first chapter.

Of course it is possible to think of situations where something which is usually thought of as being good turns out not to be good. Not even altruism is always good. There are situations where, without being an egoist, after fair and impartial consideration, one is not only justified, but duty-bound, to give one's own wishes preference over those of another person. 'Love your neighbour as yourself' does not mean 'Love him as something more important than anything else', but that when it comes to willing the good, you should make no difference between yourself and your neighbour. Anyone who actually manages that much is doing pretty well. The naturalistic fallacy consists in ascribing to the word 'good' some specific content which it does not actually possess. This does not work because of the fact that the moral perspective, the perspective of the good, is an absolute perspective, as we also saw in the first chapter. It does not make sense to say, 'It would indeed be good to do such and such, but at the moment the good is just going to have to wait'. The good is the one thing which should never and must never be made to wait. But every single individual value or content must, so it seems, be made to wait under certain circumstances, that is, when confronted with some higher value, some more pressing duty or more fundamental obligation. That is why the moral point of view is not just one additional point of view which has to be taken into account along with other, more basic points of view, when we are thinking about how to act. It is nothing less that the correct way of ordering these more basic points of view, and the one most in keeping with reality.

In this sense morality is identical to the 'objectivity' which the philosopher H. E. Hengstenberg writes about. A good action is one which does justice to reality. This answer seems very formal, if not empty. It does not seem to help very much with respect to the question of what we are supposed to do in individual cases. But the answer does not in fact claim to do this. It leads us to reconsider the actual content of our actions from a quite different point of view. It refers us back to the feeling for values which was made accessible to us during the course of our earlier development; it refers us back to the knowledge experience has given us. Doctors are taught their duty primarily by the study and practice of medicine itself. The rest they learn from the medical ethos which arises out of the nature of the relationship of trust which exists between the patient and themselves.

The largest barrier to objective judgment about what we should and should not do arises out of unwillingness, at the moment of judgment, to regard the point of view of our own selfish interests as only one point of view amongst many. That is why the oldest and most common moral rule of thumb says, 'What you don't want to be done to you, you should not do to anyone else'. In the Gospel, this rule, the so-called Golden Rule, is put, 'Do unto others as you would have them do unto you'. Kant's famous categorical imperative is basically nothing more than a refinement of this rule. It requires us to regard the principles we follow as being independent of the fact that it is we ourselves who are doing the actions and that others are on the receiving end of them. It requires us to ask ourselves if we would want all people to follow a particular rule even if we were on the receiving end. It is not my intention to discuss here the range and effectiveness of the Golden Rule and similar rules involving univeralization. Bernard Shaw once wrote, 'Do not do unto others what you would have them do unto you. Their tastes may not be the same'. All that the principle of universalization can really do is to make sure that judgments regarding one's own interests are impartial. But the test is only negative. Not all actions which pass the test are necessarily good ones. In fact all the test really rules out is a sort of primitive egoism.

The important thing when it come to deciding whether or not an action is good is something rather different. What is important is that we treat things, plants, animals, human beings and, finally, ourselves, according to the values or sets of values appropriate to them, in other words that we should deal fairly with reality. This means that it is of primary importance that we should treat all human beings as though they were every bit as much ends-in-themselves as we consider ourselves to be. Of course we need each other all the time as means to other ends. The whole of our civilization, built, as it is, upon the principle of the division of labour, depends on this fact. Only the important thing in this system is that no one should ever be just a means without at the same time being an end, that is to say, within the framework of actions and transactions, no one should be precluded from being able also to pursue their own ends.

That is why Kant said that human beings do not have value, but dignity. This is because all values are commensurable. One value can be measured against others. 'Dignity' on the other hand is the name we give to a characteristic which leads us to rule out the possibility of involving another being in this sort of trade-off. This is because that being is by nature the standard according to which values are judged, the means by which calculations about values are made. The dignity of man is connected with the idea of man being, as I said in the previous chapter, a meaningful whole, a kind of self-contained universality. A person's dignity is grounded in the fact that he is not just one aspect of reality amongst others, but that he is urged by his conscience to deal justly with reality. As a potentially moral being, a person deserves unconditional respect.

That is why we have a duty to respect ourselves. Moreover it is this respect we owe to ourselves which requires us to deal fairly also with the reality which lies outside us. For example, a person who keeps animals for his own use or pleasure owes it to himself to allow these animals to live, so long as they are alive, in a way which is appropriate to each animal. If an object can be used in a worthwhile way, the destruction of that object or the use of it in a less worthwhile way needs at least to be justified. The right of ownership is not in itself sufficient justification. All ownership does is to withdraw an object from use by others and to give the owner the right to decide upon its use. Yet that does not mean that the uses to which it is put cannot be moral or immoral. It is always immoral to throw away something which could be of use to someone else. Many people have a certain, almost superstitious aversion about throwing bread away. This aversion can easily be traced back to the fact that in earlier times bread was in short supply. But what can we deduce from this? We could come to the conclusion that abundance beyond a certain point is not good for human beings because it makes them blind to the value-content of things.

The question was 'What makes an action good?'. The answer we have now is that an action is good if it can be justified in terms of what it is. There is always something unsatisfactory about answers of this nature. They are bland and they have no practical application. They do not tell us what we should do in individual cases. Yet that is not actually necessary, because in the vast majority of individual cases we actually do know what we ought to do. The most important aspect of this sort of deliberation is that it helps us to give an account of what we already know. In most cases what we should do becomes clear from what we call the 'nature of the situation'.

It is in the very nature of a promise that it should be kept. Other people rely on one's doing so. The whole purpose of making promises is that people should be able to rely on them. It becomes clear from the very nature of small children that they need those in charge of them to give them what they need, unless they are prevented from doing so by hardship. Leaving one's own children to lead the lives of 'latch-key children' in order to be able to study social psychology and attend lectures about latch-key children simply does not make sense in terms of what we called 'the nature of the situation'.

I said that in the vast majority of cases what we should do is obvious. Yet there are times when conflicts arise and duties collide. There are times when it is right not to keep a promise because other more pressing or more important considerations justify not keeping it. With simple model situations it is easy to be sure of what to do. Yet most situations in which we find ourselves are complex. In such situations different demands are placed upon us, different responsibilities overlap, and we have to deal fairly with all of them. Even in these cases though an order of priority regarding importance and urgency can usually be established which would be obvious to any rational and right-thinking person. But this is not always the case. The extent of our own responsibilities is obviously not something which is fixed once and for all. We have already seen that it is senseless to identify this range of responsibilities with the whole world and the whole of humanity, making ourselves responsible for all the consequences of all our actions and omissions. What we actually are responsible for depends on a large number of circumstances, one of which is the sort of person we are. That is why it is not possible to establish a definitive upper limit to the question of what it is that makes an action good. In most cases it would have been possible to do something better than what an individual person actually did do. And yet it would be wrong to say that one is always duty-bound to do the best possible thing. That is simply not possible.

Still it is possible to establish a bottom-line. There are some actions which always harm human dignity and which always violate the nature of a person as an end-in-himself. These actions cannot be justified by appeal to any so-called higher or more comprehensive duties. This is connected with the fact that the human person is not pure intellect or spirit; human personality is manifest in specific ways, through body and language. If body and language are not respected as the means by which the person is represented, but are used as means to other ends, then the person is used only as a means. It follows quite obviously from this that the direct and intentional killing of another human being, torture, rape or the exploitation of sexuality as a means to certain ends is always bad. Also it is not possible to justify lying to a person who has placed his full trust in us. If we do so, we use language as a mere tool and reduce ourselves, as persons using language and represented by language, to a state where we have, in a way, disappeared as persons. Apart from that we will be depriving others of the opportunity of dealing fairly with reality, because we will be deliberately separating that other person off from reality. That is why no one should have the right to lie to a sick person, so long as that person is seriously and trustingly asking about his state of health. Lying would deprive that person of the opportunity to come to terms with his fate.

This bottom line of what is permissible is not enough to give us a definition of what a good action is. Not everyone telling the truth is necessarily doing a good action. Truth can be told with love and goodwill, and it can be used as a weapon, with malicious intent. Good intention alone, as we saw, is not enough, in itself, to make an action good. But without good intentions, or good purposes, there are no good actions. In fact more good actions, actions which are good in an unqualified way, actually do happen than we generally believe. It is worth keeping a look out for them; nothing is more cheering than coming across examples. I do not mean heroic examples, but simple things like when I asked a young man how to get somewhere which turned out not to be all that easy to find. He stopped whatever it was he was doing and walked with me for five minutes, to show me the way. This was a small incident, hardly worth talking about, but it was a fine thing to do, and that can be said without qualification. Actions like that make life worthwhile. The young man did not indulge in any great moral reflections, he simply did what occured to him to do; and this occured to him because of the sort of person he was.

The medieval philosophers had an old saying, *agere sequitur esse*, 'action follows out of being'. Of course not only actions can be good, but people are. In the Christian tradition it is love that makes people good. This is a fundamentally affirmative attitude towards reality. It is out of love that universal goodwill arises. In terms of this universal goodwill we no longer stand in the middle of the world; universal goodwill reaches out to include us. We need to live in a state of friendship with ourselves, if we are to live well. However, if we measure ourselves against this standard of love, we see ourselves as being good only in a conditional way.

I said before that what the good is in a particular situation, depends, amongst other things, on the characteristics of the person in that situation. If someone has been injured on a ship people ask if there is a doctor on board. If there is, the doctor is under an obligation to help. There are similar implications regarding other human characteristics. Some people are more far-sighted than others. They owe it to others under certain circumstances to give good advice. Some people have a more highly developed sense of values. One might well reproach these people for doing certain things one would never dream of holding against others. Some people have to accept reponsibilities on behalf of others who would not see themselves as being responsible in the same way. This is because the former have simply seen something the others have failed to see.

Action follows out of being. There is no doubt that there are hierarchical differences of status, between people, as well as between values. Some people are on a higher moral plane than others. This is not because they are in some way permitted to do more, but because they have to do more, since they are more capable and since they see more and understand better. These people do not generally seem to themselves to be better than others, in fact the discrepancy between what they see and what they are actually able to do is so great that they are more likely to suffer as a result. They simply have a more refined conscience. Christianity has always been accused of implanting feelings of guilt into people. That is just about as right as it is wrong. The truth of the matter is that Christianity has sharpened our sense of value and made us better at seeing reality. Accordingly it has reduced the possibility of our innocently doing wrong or innocently failing to do good. Where there is more light, shadows are more evident. We all cast shadows. 'No one is good but God alone' says the New Testament. The Greek philosopher Anaximander, living centuries earlier, was already aware of this. He wrote, 'All things fade away and return to the stuff out of which they came into being, all in the fullness of time; as such they do penance to one another for injustice'. What Anaximander meant by this was that everything which exists occupies space which it takes away from other things. It becomes guilty simply because it exists and pays for its guilt by having, after a certain length of time, to make room for other things.

Even if we cannot go along with the mythological idea of things being guilty merely as a result of their existence, it is still a fact that no one is able to free himself totally from his own egocentric point of view. We all have our blind spots, our built-in inabilities to see certain things, and there is a way in which we all tread on each other's toes. That is why no one can draw a precise line between guilt and innocence. Lack of awareness, which is the root of evil, depends on our repressing certain things. Whether we forget intentionally or unintentionally, we become guilty towards one another.

However, there is more to it than just an unpitying wheel of justice, constantly exacting payment from people and from things. Human beings are capable of acknowledging their own limitations as guilt, imputing ignorance to others and forgiving them. There is not only justice, there is also forgiveness and reconciliation. No amount of good actions alter the fact that there is no such thing as a human life which as a whole is worthy of being called good without qualification. Everyone needs forbearance and perhaps even forgiveness. But the only sort of person who is really worthy to lay claim to this for himself is one who, without closing his eyes to evil that has been done, is ready to forgive unconditionally. Forbearance, forgiveness and reconciliation constitute a higher form of justice. This is

what Hegel was referring to when he wrote, 'The wounds
of the spirit heal without leaving scars'.

Chapter eight

Equanimity: our attitude to what we cannot change

The next topic does not often crop up in modern works on ethics. At first sight it does not seem to belong to the realm of ethics at all; the topic is 'destiny'. Ethics has to do with our actions, with what is determined by us. It may seem that something which, by its very nature, exists outside us cannot possibly be an object of ethical reflection. Yet, again and again, thinkers throughout history have considered that the most important thing for man is that he should establish a correct relationship between himself and that which exists independently of him, with destiny. Hegel wrote in his 'Habilitationsthesen' (cf. Hegel, *Werke*, II: 533) that, 'The starting point, the first principle in the study of morals, is the respect we have to show towards destiny'. ('Principium scientiae moralis est reverentia fato habenda.')

How should we understand this? Why should we bother to make something we cannot influence the object of practical deliberation, since, in practice, such deliberation would appear to be without consequence? Let us look first at the answer that the dignity of human actions consists, as we have seen, in the fact that they do not simply fit into an overriding framework of events as if they were unthinking components. Every human life is itself a meaningful whole. There is a sense in which each individual is unconditionally responsible for his own actions. Even if a person is acting only tentatively or experimentally, or if he is unable to foresee the consequences of his actions, the fact that there are certain things which at certain times he either has done or has not done, is still an inescapable fact.

As such these things will always be an integral part of that person's life and it is in this way that he is responsible for them.

But how can we be responsible if we know all along that our every action is in fact only a component part of a more comprehensive system of events, over which we have no control? If human freedom is understood as absolute independence, then there is only one action left to us: suicide. By means of suicide we remove ourselves from the workings of the world. But this action negates freedom at the very moment it brings it about. Freedom is consumed by suicide because afterwards it no longer exists.

Furthermore, anyone who acts no longer has the choice as to whether or not they wish to establish a relationship with reality. The fact of acting in itself establishes such a relationship. As soon as a person begins to act he has already accepted destiny, past as well as future. This is because human beings are not capable of acting in a void or *ex nihilo*, so the whole concept of action always includes the idea of accepting certain conditions. Politics is a good example. There are so-called politicians who declare that they are not able to implement the policies they would *really* like to, because the conditions are not right. People like that have no idea what political action really is. Political action always means doing whatever makes most sense given the conditions, even if we did not choose them, or in other words, doing the best possible thing under the circumstances. Of course this may involve trying to change the circumstances.

Man is different from animals in that he can change the nature of the limitations to his actions by action itself. This is what history is all about. Yet this is only possible if we initially accept a given framework for our actions. Anyone who is unable or unwilling to do this is still in an infantile state. These conditions consist not only in the exterior framework of our actions, but also in the way we are at the time, our own nature, our biography. Not only is reality outside us just the way it is, we too are to a certain extent the way we are without being able to change. Of course it is a bad excuse for a person who has just wronged another to say, 'but that's the way I am'. The way we are does not have fixed proportions which determine the way we act. On the contrary, the way we are is formed and re-formed by the way we act. Yet these actions do not arise out of nothing. It is not possible for us to do all things at all times.

Only during the course of our life do we discover the limitations which our nature prescribes. If it is true that with every action we influence and form ourselves indirectly, then it is also true that our past actions take on the character of destiny for us. This is an important consideration, because a vital aspect of right living is clear consciousness of the fact that everything we do, every word, every gesture, everything we read, every television programme we watch, everything we fail to do, is an irrevocable element of the way we are formed. The relative value of something can change, and we can start off in a new direction, but nothing is ever the same as it was before. In the course of time our own action takes on the character of destiny. Anyone who does not want that to happen should not act at all. But that would not help either, since such a person's decision not to act would also become part of his destiny.

Even more irritating for our sense of our own autonomy is the fact that a person who acts cannot control the future either. Indeed a person is only really able to act if he is ready to acquiesce to destiny as far as the future is concerned. It is easy to understand why. It is simply because of the fact that we are unable to control the long-term consequences of our actions. Even the chess player, when matched against someone of similar ability to himself, is unable to predict the way a game will go. Each one of his moves represents a challenge to his opponent to make a counter-move, and this counter-move is not just a component part of his overall strategy. In the long term we do not know what the results of our actions will be. We can hope that our best intentions will be taken up by those who come after us and in some way continued. We represent destiny to them just as much as they do to us. We cannot hold this destiny in our hands.

That is why action always implies letting ourselves go, freeing ourselves and our intentions from any hope of total control. As such, finite action is a kind of training for death. In reality there is no clear dividing line between action and suffering. The endurance of suffering is always implied by the idea of action. So if the life of an individual is to be a meaningful whole, suffering itself must, conversely, be seen as a form of action. There are two possibilities. We can either see our actions as being absorbed and neutralized by the exterior reality of destiny, like the concentric ripples made by a stone dropped in a large lake, or else we can try to establish a conscious and explicit relationship with what happens, and as such include it in the meaning of our life.

What would this look like? What sort of a relationship can we establish between ourselves and what happens? It seems to me that there are three possibilities. To describe them I shall use the words fanaticism, cynicism and equanimity.

The fanatic adheres to the principle that the only sense there is in things is put there and made real by us. He simply refuses to accept the fact that anyone who acts is opposed by the superior forces of destiny. He wants either to change the basic framework of the conditions of reality or to be destroyed. Michael Kohlhaas becomes a fanatic. He is not ready to accept his own powerlessness in face of the injustice committed against him and is prepared to set the whole world ablaze in order that justice should be done. Every revolutionary is a fanatic, so long as he recognizes no moral limits to his actions, because he thinks that it is only through his actions that any sense can come into the world at all. Every moral point of view by contrast starts from the position that there is already sense in the world, and that this sense results from the existence of each individual person. If this were not the case, any attempt to do anything meaningful would be in vain. The fanatic is the person who like Hitler thinks that if he and his like are destroyed, then the sense of world history is lost.

The opposite of the fanatic is the cynic, although in practice they are confusingly similar to one another. The cynic does not join sides with sense against reality, but with reality against sense. He is not interested in sense. He sees actions in terms of mechanical events. He believes in the right of the strongest. The Athenians were acting cynically when they took it upon themselves to blackmail the small island of Melos into becoming their allies against the Spartans. They threatened to kill all the men and to take all the women and children into slavery. The Melesians pointed out the injustice of this. But the Athenians answered, 'What is the meaning of justice here? There can only be justice between two parties of similar strength. You are weak, we are strong, and all else follows from this.' That is cynicism, unadulterated by any ideology, for ideology constitutes at least a formal recognition of moral rules, like those of justice, even if those rules are distorted to serve particular interests. It is possible to have different views about individual ideologies. One can try to expose them, criticize them or take them at their word. It is not possible to argue against the cynic however, because he has already taken up the position that there is no sense in reality. The fanatic is, so to speak, foaming at the mouth; the cynic grins. After a while, the fanatic often becomes a cynic, that is, if he finally comes round to an experience of the superiority of the reality he has been fighting. They are in basic agreement with one another from the beginning that the reality in the context of which our actions take place, out of which they arise and into which they are channelled, is fundamentally without sense.

This is enough to demonstrate that action can only be meaningful if a positive relationship is established with reality, so as to provide a framework in the context of which we can act. It may perhaps be possible to explain this to the fanatic who is actually looking for meaning, but not to the cynic. The cynic is no more susceptible to argument than the radical sceptic. The cynic can only be left to his own devices and must be opposed if there is a risk of his harming others. The only way such a person could probably be helped would be for someone to show him meaning in the world or lead him to experience value in some way other than by means of argument. Love may perhaps help him, but only if he wants to be helped, and only if he sees that cynicism is a sickness which deprives a person of seeing any sense in life.

The reasonable attitude for a person to adopt towards destiny, an attitude which has been taught by the philosophy of all times, is what we call equanimity. The German word, *Gelassenheit,* comes from the language of medieval German mysticism, but the idea is very simple. By equanimity we mean the attitude of someone who regards what he cannot change as a meaningful limit to his ability to act and who accepts this limit. That seems to be trivial. What is going to happen is going to happen anyway, whether we accept it or not. True. Yet this is why we have to be reconciled with it, for otherwise we cannot be reconciled with ourselves. For our very existence, who we are and what we are, is destiny. Whoever is unable to accept destiny is unable to accept himself. Unless one can live in friendship with oneself it is not possible to lead a good life.

It was above all the Stoic philosophers who developed the teaching of equanimity. Epictetus and Seneca prized the acceptance of destiny as man's ultimate liberation. They said that if you assume into your will whatever happens, nothing can ever happen to you against your will. You are as free as God. The highest ideal of Stoicism was *apathia,* a state free from suffering and free from passion. It is possible to object against this position that it deprives human action of an important dimension, that of passionate commitment. The Stoics taught freedom from passion and condemned even feelings of pity. They thought that man should act out of pure moral reasoning alone. But passions are part of human nature and the Stoic is keen to accept nature. So in fact he really ought to accept his own nature. Apart from that it is only someone acting in a committed way who is able to test out the limits of what is possible. If he gives way because he is faced with the impossible then he knows that it really was impossible; though it certainly is more painful for him to give up than for the Stoic, because he is having to renounce something which he really was committed to.

At this point Christian ethics part company with Stoical ethics. Christianity teaches, like all other moral and religious teachings throughout the world, that we should submit to destiny. At the same time though it is different from other teachings, first because of its greater realism and also because it embodies a new kind of motivation. The realism lies in the fact that the limits imposed by our natural subjectivity really are taken into account. The person who has this sort of equanimity does not deceive the gods by declaring that the grapes which they refuse him are too sour anyway. He is not free from passion, nor is he indifferent to the success or failure of his intentions in the way that the Stoics say one should be. That is why his failure is the more dramatic. In the Old Testament we have a description of Job's quarrel with God, his desperate complaints against God. He is able to make these complaints because, unlike the cynic, Job insists that reality, being a work of God, must be meaningful. But he cannot discover this meaning. At the end we learn of his simple capitulation before the superior power of God. God points out that when all is said and done it was He, and not Job, who made the crocodile and the hippopotamus. Jesus too is obviously somebody quite different from a Stoic sage, when, gripped with the fear of death, he begs for his life, and then adds, 'Not my will, but Your will be done'.

Resignation to the inevitable is only truly human if what we consider to be inevitable has actually been shown to be just that. Yet this can only be done if we are prepared to go to the very limits; not if we are so scared of getting a few boils that we make no effort to broaden the range of what is possible. That is why equanimity is not the same as fatalism. It is the readiness of an agent to accept his own failure as something significant. This of course presupposes that we do not *a priori* draw a line between our actions and the reality which on the one hand makes action possible and on the other brings about its failure.

Religion is characterized by the fact that it sees both possibilities as having the same cause. On the one hand God is seen as the source and guarantor of moral obligation. On the other hand He is seen as the Lord of History; that is to say that He is still honoured even if our good intentions fail and, what is more, He is seen as a guarantee that good intentions will ultimately be reconciled with the course of history. This latter is most important. We could imagine, by way of analogy, the opposite possibility, an evil spirit or spirit of deceit, like the one Descartes invented, which would systematically arrange for all our good intentions always to be turned to opposite effect so that our good actions always produced bad effects. In such a world good actions would not be possible.

That is why good action requires trust that the world is not actually like that, trust that good leads to good, at least if one takes a long-term, general view. It is only then that there can be any sense at all in a good action; it is only then that the good one might see in it escapes destruction by the course of history. Yet we can only believe this if we believe also that it is not possible for evil successfully to prevail in any definitive way; for in that case all good intentions would have ultimately to be seen as redundant. That is why a belief in God also includes the idea that, in the long term, bad intentions are turned to opposite effect and have in some way to contribute to the good. Of course this sort of idea lies at the heart of the philosophies of history put forward by Kant and Fichte as well as by Hegel and, naturally, Marx. This is why Goethe, in his *Faust*, has Mephisto define himself as follows, 'I am a part of that power, which always wants evil, yet always brings about good'.

A person who has equanimity acts decisively. At the same time though he accepts the course of events which have made his action possible, and this involves also accepting the possibility of failure; he knows that meaning in the world does not depend only on him and his actions. Martin Luther mentions a missionary who wanted to convert a country but did not actually succeed in converting a single person. He begins to complain about his fate. Luther rebukes him with the following observation, 'It is a sure sign of a bad will that it cannot tolerate being frustrated'.

In this sense equanimity does not mean passivity or giving up hope of changing the world. It is rather an affirmation of reality, which is seen as valuable enough for it to be worth our while coming to its aid by trying to change it. If the most important things about the world could be summed up by saying that the world is bad, it would not be worthwhile bringing people into the world, for every human being is a new means by which the world is brought to consciousness. A world which was essentially bad though would not be worth bringing to consciousness, for there it would just be reflected, over and over again. Therefore everything anyone ever does to help another, indeed all social activity, only makes sense to the extent that it leads people to discover that life is worth living. It has to be said of course that there are conditions where this discovery is almost impossible.

Accepting reality with equanimity is, as we have seen, necessary if man is to live in harmony with the world, with his fellow human beings and with himself, that is to say, it is the condition for a happy life. It is also necessary if our subjective sense of the meaning of life is not to be belied by reality. One last consideration should make this clear. I have already said that different generations are to one another as destiny. We take over the world in the state in which it was left us by the previous generation. This reminds us that the next generation will in some way or other come to take over the inheritance we leave them and carry on with our intentions. Friendship between generations then is necessary to ensure that this destiny, which embraces the actions of both generations, should not prove hostile. The older generation has the duty on the one hand to initiate the younger into its sets of values so that the young should be able to understand them, and so that they should be able to see their own actions as a continuation of the actions of those who came before them. But the older generation also has the task of leaving the world to those who come after them in such a state that the latter should be able to do something useful with their inheritance, so that they should not find themselves confronted either with an overwhelming infrastructure which they can never feel part of, or on the other hand with an inheritance which has been decimated and plundered. The young can only act in a meaningful way if they can establish a positive relationship with the reality, albeit the incomplete reality, they find before them.

There is of course no substitute for equanimity. This is true in all circumstances, particularly in bad circumstances, though of course it is not always easy to achieve. It is one of the fundamental duties of man to his fellow men to make it easier for them to accept reality with equanimity. Duty is probably the wrong word here. A happy man has a natural need to share his happiness. A joy shared is, as they say, a joy doubled. Equanimity is a quality of the happy man. The philosopher Wittgenstein goes so far as to write, 'I am either happy or unhappy. One could say that there is no such thing as Good and Evil'. That is put probably too succinctly and is open to misinterpretation. What Wittgenstein meant was perhaps put better by the philosopher and optical lens grinder Spinoza who wrote, 'Happiness is not the reward of virtue, virtue itself is'.

Select bibliography

Anaximander (1960) 'Fragmente', in H. Diels (ed.), *Fragmente der Vorsokratiker*, I, Berlin.

Aristoteles (1960) 'Nikomachische Ethik', II, Berlin: I. Bekker.

Claudius, Matthias (1968) 'Brief an meinen Sohn Johannes' (1799), in *Sämtliche Werke*, München: Winkler-Verlag.

Descartes, René (1904) 'Meditationen', in C. Adam and P. Tannéry (eds), *Oeuvres*, VII, Paris.

Freud, Sigmund (1969) 'Jenseits des Lustprinzips', *Gesammelte Werke*, XIII, Frankfurt am Main.

Hegel, G. W. F. (1986) *Grundlinien der Philosophie des Rechts oder Naturrecht und Staatswissenschaft im Grundrisse*, Frankfurt am Main: Suhrkamp.

Hegel, G. W. F. (1970) *Werke*, II, Frankfurt am Main: Suhrkamp.

Hengstenberg, Hans Eduard (1969) *Grundlegung der Ethik*, Stuttgart.

Kant, I. (1903/11) *Grundlegung zur Metaphysik der Sitten*, Akad.-Ausg., IV, Berlin.

Kant, I. (1912/23) *Über ein vermeintliches Recht aus Menschenliebe zu lügen*, Akad.-Ausg., VIII, Berlin.

Luther, Martin (1951) 'Zwei Fastenpredigten Luthers vom 15. u. 17. März 1518, in Borcherdt and Merz (eds), *Ausgewählte Werke*, München.

Marx, Karl (1962) 'Kritik des Gothaer Programms', in *Marx Engels Werke*, 19, Berlin.

Mitscherlich, A. and M. (1968) *Die Unfähigkeit zu trauern*, München.

Plato (1953ff.) *Gorgias*, III, Oxford: Burnet. *Philebos*, II, Burnet. *Politeia*, IV, Burnet. *Briefe*, V, Burnet.

Rousseau, Jean-Jacques (1969) *Emile*, in *Oeuvres complètes*, IV, Paris: Pléjade.

Scheler, Max (1954) *Der Formalismus in der Ethik und die materiale Wertethik*, Bern.

Seneca (1949) *Epistulae morales*, 2 vols, 2 editions, Roma: Achilles Beltrami.

Spinoza, B. de (1972) *Ethica,* ed. C. Gebhard, II, Heidelberg.

Weber, Max (1971) 'Politik als Beruf', in *Gesammelte politische Schriften,* Tübingen: J. F. Winckelmann.

Wittgenstein, Ludwig (1960) 'Tagebücher', in *Schriften,* I, Frankfurt am Main.

Translator's bibliography

This bibliography gives references to works dealing with the background or further arguments relevant to the ideas in the corresponding chapters of Professor Spaemann's *Basic Moral Concepts*. Where appropriate I have included works most at odds with Professor Spaemann's views at the end of the relevant list.

Chapter one

Williams, B. (1985) *Ethics and the Limits of Philosophy*, London: Fontana.

McIntyre, A. (1981) *After Virtue*, London: Duckworth.

Murdoch, I. (1970) *The Sovereignty of Good*, London: Routledge & Kegan Paul.

Mackie, J. (1977) *Ethics: Inventing Right and Wrong*, New York: Penguin.

Young, M. F. D. (1972) *Knowledge and Control*, London: Collier.

Chapter two

Freud, S. (1950) *Dictionary of Psychoanalysis*, trans. and ed. N. Fordor, London: Greenwood Press.

Freud, S. (1984) *Beyond the Pleasure Principle*, ed. A. Dickinson, London: Penguin.

McIntyre, A. (1976) *Unconscious*, London: Routledge & Kegan Paul.

Dearden, R. F. (1972) 'Happiness and Education' in R. F. Dearden, *et al.*, (eds) *Education and the Development of Reason*, London: Routledge & Kegan Paul.

Chapter three

Weil, S. (1951) *Waiting on God*, trans. Emma Cranford, London: Routledge & Kegan Paul.

Kenny, A. (1985) *Aquinas*, 'Past Masters' series, Oxford: Oxford University Press.

White, J. P. (1982) *The Aims of Education Restated*, London: Routledge & Kegan Paul.

Warnock, M. (1977) *Schools of Thought*, London: Faber.

Sartre, J. P. (1974) *Existentialism and Humanism*, trans. P. Mairet, London: Methuen.

Chapter four

Plato (1971) *Gorgias*, trans. W. Hamilton, London: Penguin.

Rawls, J. (1972) *A Theory of Justice*, Oxford: Oxford University Press.

Marx, K. (1978) *Critique of the Gotha Program*, London: Central Books.

Nozick, R. (1978) *Anarchy State and Utopia*, Oxford: Blackwell.

Taylor, C. (1982) 'The Nature and Scope of Distributive Justice' in *Philosophy and the Human Sciences Philosophical Papers 2*.

Chapter five

Smart, J. C. C. and Williams, B. (1973) *Utilitarianism For and Against*, Cambridge: Cambridge University Press.

Waldron, J. (ed.) (1984) *Theories of Rights*, Oxford: Oxford University Press.

Sen, A. and Williams, B. (eds) (1982) *Utilitarianism and Beyond*, Cambridge: Cambridge University Press.

Hare, R. M. (1981) *Moral Thinking*, Oxford: Oxford University Press.

Mill, J. S. (1861) *Utilitarianism*, ed. M. Warnock (1962), London: Fontana.

Chapter six

Murdoch, I. (1970) *The Sovereignty of Good*, London: Routledge & Kegan Paul.

Kant, I. (1948) *The Moral Law*, trans. H. J. Paton, London: Hutchinson.

Hildebrand, D. von (1953) *Christian Ethics*, London: Thames & Hudson.

D'Arcy, E. (1961) *Conscience and its Right to Freedom*, London: Sheed & Ward.

Nagel, T. (1979) 'Moral Luck' in *Mortal Questions*, Cambridge: Cambridge University Press.

Chapter seven

Finlay, I. H. (1982) *Anaximander Fragment,* London: Wild Hawthorn Press.

Norman, R. (1983) *An Introduction to Ethics,* Oxford: Clarendon.

Acton, H. B. (1970) *Kant's Moral Philosophy,* London: Macmillan.

Paton, H. J. (1947) *The Categorical Imperative,* London: Hutchinson.

Moore, G. E. (1903) *Principiae Ethicae,* Cambridge: Cambridge University Press.

Chapter eight

Smith Cyprian, O. S. B. (1987) *The Way of Paradox: Spiritual Life as Taught by M. Eckhart,* London: Darton, Longman & Todd.

Kleist, B. H. v. (1978) *The Marquise of O. and Other Stories,* trans. D. Luke and N. Reeves, London: Penguin.

Taylor, R. (1963) *Metaphysics,* London: Prentice Hall.

Seneca (1969) *Letters from a Stoic,* trans. R. Campbell, London: Penguin.

Wittgenstein, L. (1960) 'Tagebücher' in *Schriften,* I, Frankfurt am Main.

Index